I0505174

Drawing Lessons

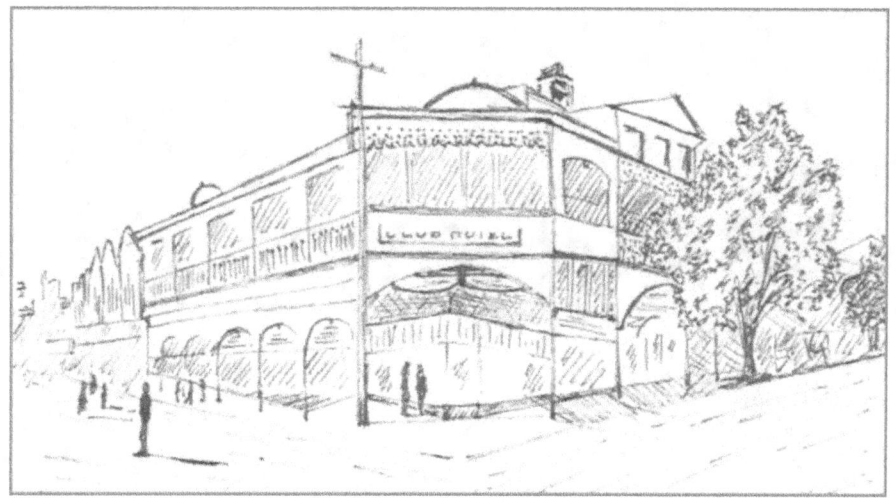

-- FOR HOBBY ARTISTS --

By KATE BERRY

Copyright © 2015 Kate Berry

All rights reserved.

ISBN-10: 1508442975
ISBN-13: 978-1508442974

DEDICATION

This book is dedicated to Jay, Tiesh, Caitlin and Brayden
– the sunshine and happiness in my life.

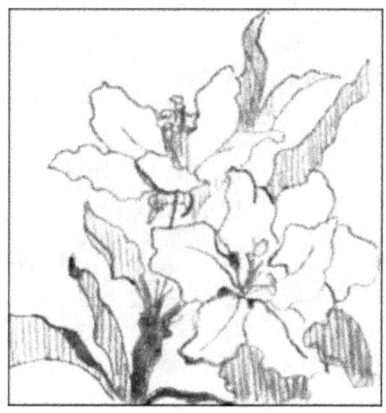

ACKNOWLEDGEMENTS

I have to thank my beautiful family (including my lovely in-laws) for their constant love and support, plus a little extra hug for my hubby.

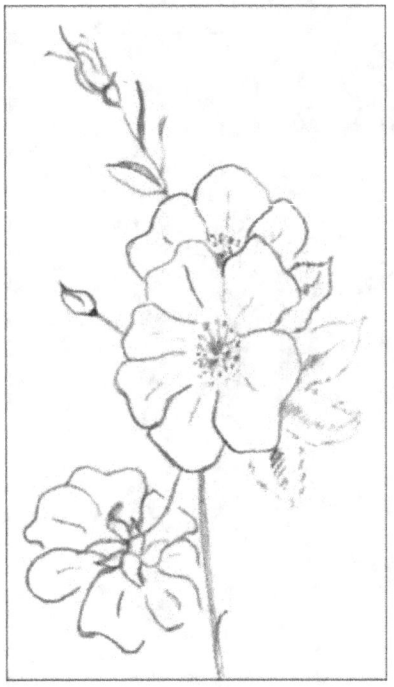

CONTENTS:

PREFACE

This edition is a combination of 4 popular Kindle books, namely:

DRAWING LESSONS

HOW TO DRAW OUTLINES

DRAWING AND SKETCHING NATURE

DRAWING TIPS FOR BEGINNERS

<u>Drawing Lessons</u> shows you how to become comfortable with a pencil; to competently draw lines in all directions; and most importantly, it encourages good eye-hand co-ordination.

<u>How To Draw Outlines</u> demonstrates a variety of ways to construct basic outlines and all you have to do is adopt the one that suits you the most.

<u>Drawing and Sketching Nature</u> adds another layer to the information shared in the previous 2 books. Using Nature as our teacher, it demonstrates how easy it is to progress with what you've learned so far.

<u>Drawing Tips for Beginners</u> wraps everything together when Kate reveals a wide variety of tricks that she used to create successful images constantly. These simple tips will work for everyone, regardless of skill level.

Starting with just a single line, you commence an exciting adventure to eventually become a very capable hobby artist.

01 - DRAWING LESSONS – BOOK 1

INTRODUCTION

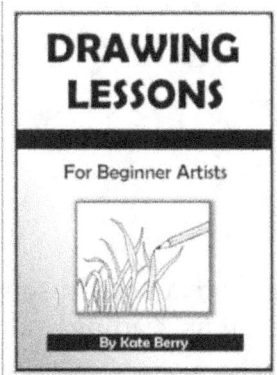

Nature is the best Art Teacher you will ever find. When we draw or sketch from Nature, a wonderful variety of scenery is brought to our attention and we learn to notice things that we normally take for granted.

We also gain the ability to:

* compare different characteristics,

* discriminate and exercise judgment,

* test and strengthen our memory.

It is these new talents that take us into a world of wonders that lies beyond our normal world.

So, the question is, *how do we arrive at this special place where the pencil dances over the paper with a mind of its own?*

Well, first you have to acquire good hand/eye co-ordination and this is done with the easy little practice sessions that are described here in great detail.

If you can't draw a vase of flowers indoors, then you are not likely to have much success drawing or sketching directly from Nature outdoors. However, once you do the preliminary practice similar to the type demonstrated here, you are armed with confidence and enthusiasm and you're good to go.

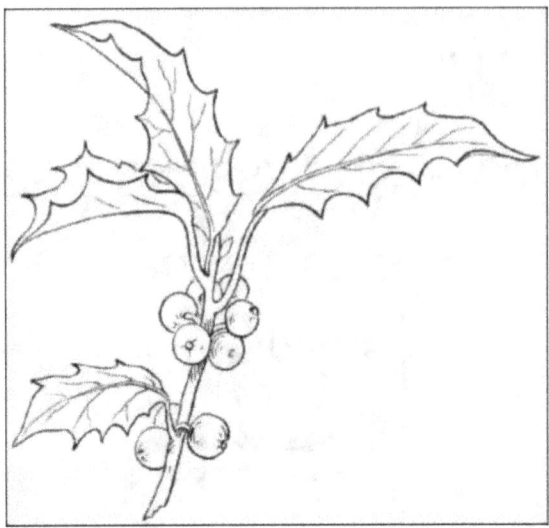

This instruction was used by teachers in schools many years ago, when art was considered as important as reading and writing.

Sometimes, vital information gets lost in the fast pace of life but by reading this book and taking action, you are not going to be one of those who missed out!

Our ultimate aim is to learn to draw efficiently and one major factor towards that goal is in these pages.

My pencil of choice for drawing or sketching is a 2B mechanical pencil so I use it when practicing, too. I also use A4 photocopy paper and fill at least one sheet for each practice exercise.

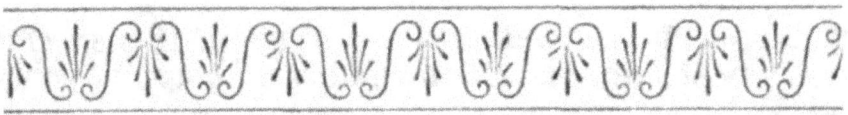

02 - STRAIGHT LINES

EXERCISE ONE

The first simple exercise is a study of parallel straight lines. It's very convenient to draw a reasonably straight line whenever you want so this tip will be good for life.

We are going to create our own square structure for this exercise, but if you prefer, you can save some time with feint-ruled paper.

The square measures roughly 2" x 2" (5cm x 5cm) but it doesn't matter if it isn't exact.

TIP: Use the sides of paper to help you reference a straight line.

Steps to produce a freehand square:

1. Along the top, mark in 3 dots about one inch (2.5 cm) apart, to form 2 columns.

2. Place 4 dots, one under the other and about ½ inch apart, below the first dot on the left.

3. Repeat these 4 dots under the center and right sides, as shown in Figure 1 below.

4. Connect the dots to create the box. You can use a ruler if you want, but you're missing out on half the fun!

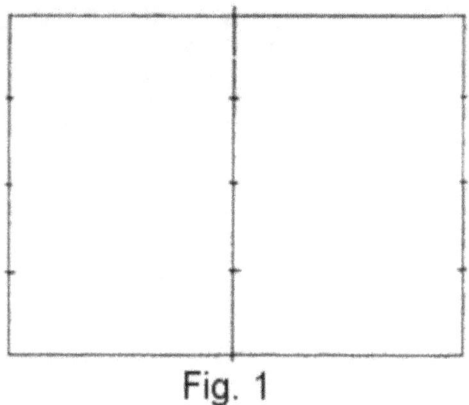

Fig. 1

You will discover your own method for placing dots to create the square, it can be done in any way, just so long as you end up with something that looks like the preceding example.

For reference purposes, a ruler was used to create Figure 1 in order to illustrate the proper diagram. So that you know I practiced what I preach, I show my <u>original</u> learning efforts throughout this section.

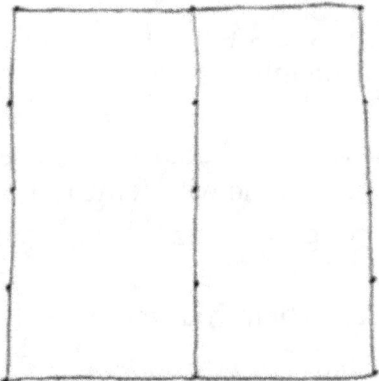

Your first couple of attempts may look pretty rough (like mine above) but as you keep going, boundaries and lines become fairly good quality.

Tip: Ignore the voice in your head that says this activity looks boring! You'll realize the long-lasting benefits for this practice later on.

I actually enjoyed the process of estimating and gauging the markers and making straight lines. Sure, some were out of place, but **after repeating the exercise a few times**, I was getting the hang of creating good lines.

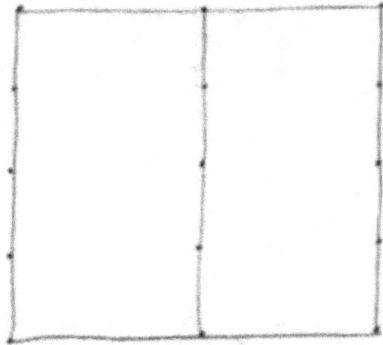

Now let's move along and use this box to practice drawing straight lines from the central point to each side, as demonstrated in the following Figure 2.

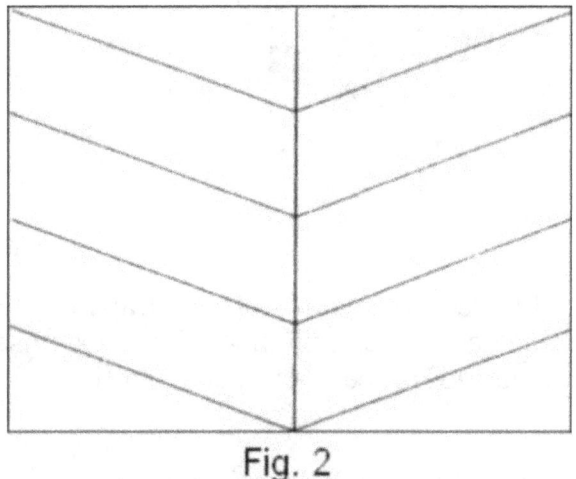

Fig. 2

The procedure:

1. Place the pencil on the first <u>middle</u> (center) dot from the top.

2. Before you move the pencil, focus on the destination dot up to the left (see example).

3. Don't watch the pencil move; keep your eye on the place where you want the pencil to arrive.

You may feel kind of awkward trying to get a straight line on one particular side but this is normal, keep persisting and ultimately your hand becomes more flexible.

Notice your improvement as you repeat this exercise and how you begin to naturally look ahead to the dot that your line is going to meet, rather than watching the pencil. This is a good, progressive step in the training of eye/hand co-ordination.

When you're not satisfied with a line, go over it again and again. The following example shows that I was getting closer to my goal of straight lines freehand.

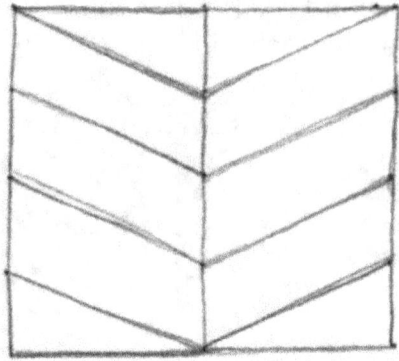

At first, it's hard to see the benefits of any drawing exercise, but if you are dedicated to the task of completing all the exercises in this book, drawing becomes a natural process and you don't have to 'remember' how to draw.

Anyway, at this stage I was elated to discover it is very possible to draw a fairly straight line!

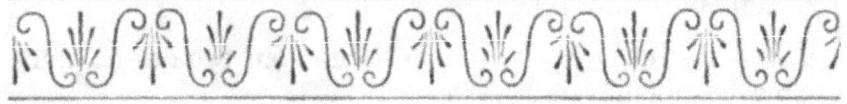

03 - CURVED LINES

EXERCISE TWO

The second exercise is similar to the previous exercise only this time we practice drawing parallel curves.

Create a square structure the same as in Exercise 1...

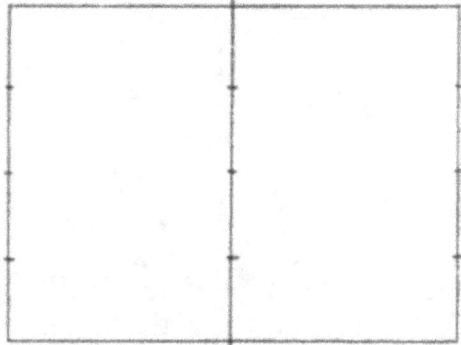

By the time you finish creating some square boundaries, you won't even be lifting your hand or pencil off the paper, your confidence increases with each and every one you do. Notice also that you instantly recognize when dots are out of place.

Now we shift our focus to mastering a nice curved line. To gain more flexibility in making curves, try resting the hand lightly on the pivot bone of the wrist as in Figure 3 below.

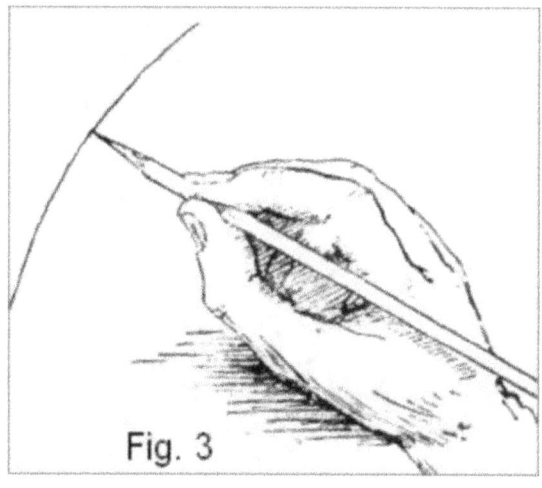

Fig. 3

Let's start practicing drawing curved lines in the box, from the central point to the left side first and then the right, as in Figure 4.

<u>TIP</u>: Start with the middle dot each time you produce a stroke. It might seem easier to start from the outside but please resist the temptation because you won't receive the ultimate benefits of this exercise.

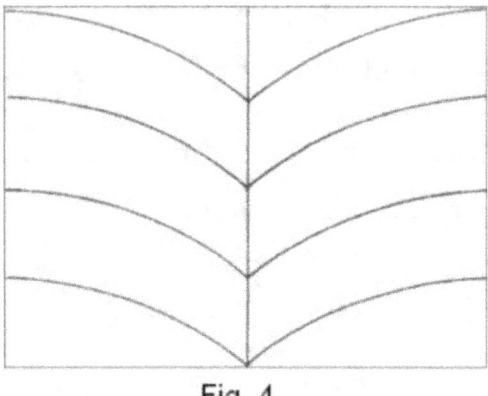

Fig. 4

To ensure a good curved line, move the pencil up and outwards from the middle dot. If your lines are too straight, try visualizing a portion of a circle for added assistance.

Compare your practice lines with Figure 4 carefully and proceed to trim them into proper shape, not by erasing, but by adding the improvements to existing lines (as in my example below). The first irregular attempt is a guide to something better.

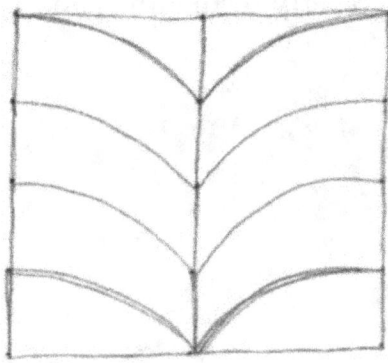

Once the curve on the left is correct, the reverse of the same curve on the right is somewhat easier because it's not a new shape, it's merely the same shape flipped over.

Now proceed to the next row and draw the curve in the same way, judging the space in between as well as the shape of the curve. Add curve by curve, taking each one on the left and then its reverse on the right, so that you adopt this succession of steps and it becomes a habit.

Keep practicing for as long as you can without becoming bored. Boredom makes you put pencils down and you're left with no yearning to pick them up again. Always protect your enthusiasm by staying interested at all times.

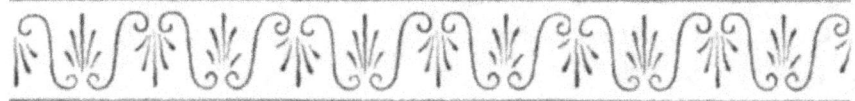

04 - SIMPLE CURVES

EXERCISE THREE

The main aim of this type of practice is to master the hand and gain a delicate touch.

Begin with the simplest lines and practice each exercise thoroughly until you overcome any difficulties you encounter.

The hand can generally make lines and curves in some directions with more ease than others but because foliage grows in all positions, we need to find the corresponding freedom with a pencil.

A simple curve is merely a bent line. Curves are needed for spirals, volutes, circles or ellipses.

Spirals:

A spiral is represented in Figure 5 and the most common illustration of it is a wire spring.

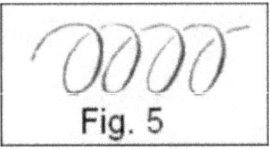

Fig. 5

By referring to the original example (Fig.5) each time, I finally realized the loops were closer together - ah ha, this kind of practice is also teaching me to see properly! By the time I finished this session, the spirals were forming effortlessly. Below is a small portion of my practice page.

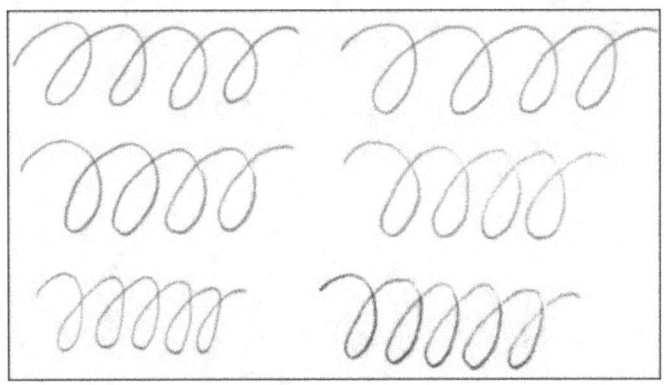

Volutes:

A volute is an evenly diminishing simple curve, or spiral, shown here in Figure 6.

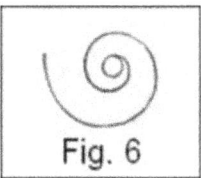

Fig. 6

Below you can see another snippet of my practice sheet, some look pretty bad but as I progressed down the page, I could feel my hand and pencil becoming synchronized.

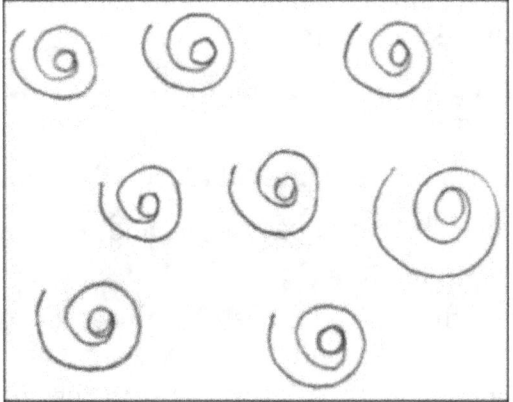

The reason I'm showing you my practice efforts is to demonstrate that we all have to start somewhere. Don't expect perfection and you won't be disappointed with your efforts at any time.

Circles:

A circle is a figure with the edge being equally distant from the center.

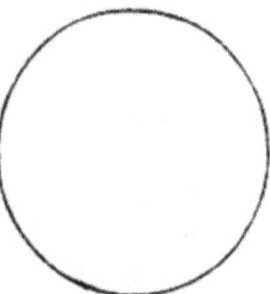

The next diagram illustrates one way to *practice* drawing circles. It's not suitable to use when you're outdoors sketching but it's great to understand another process used to create a circle.

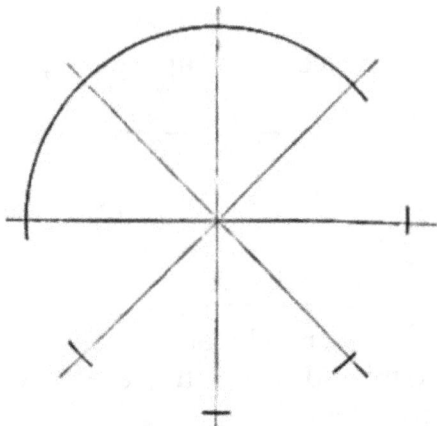

1. Draw a center line and a cross line, each any length, and use the crossing point as the center of the circle.

2. Draw through it any number of lines or at least as many as you see in the diagram above.

3. Mark off each of these lines at an equal distance from the center.

4. The curve of the circle passes through each mark and corrected as appropriate.

To start the curve, draw short lines at right angles to the first line, as shown in the diagram, and bend the curve gradually from these short marks. It helps to place the hand on the inside of the curve to draw easily.

How To Draw A Circle Freehand:

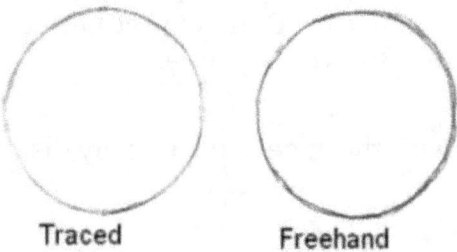

Traced   Freehand

Before we start, have a go at drawing a circle freehand so you have a before and after comparison.

Now draw another circle by going around a lid or a round object to get the "feel" of the circle and the type of stroke needed.

As soon as you do that, draw another circle only this time do it freehand, without any aids. It's better than any you have attempted before, isn't it?

I drew my freehand circle in a series of arcs. I also turned the paper around so that I was drawing the arc in the same position to help me feel the consistency of the curve.

Keep practicing by continuously going around the same circle, again and again. If you do this regularly, you will never feel reluctant to include circles in your artwork.

How to draw an Ellipse:

Figure 7 is an ellipse, which is the shape of a circle viewed at an angle.

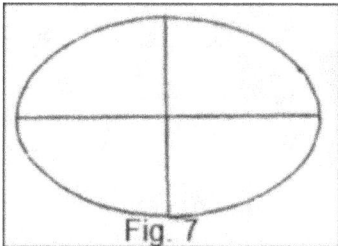

Fig. 7

First draw a horizontal line and then cross it with a <u>shorter</u> vertical line.

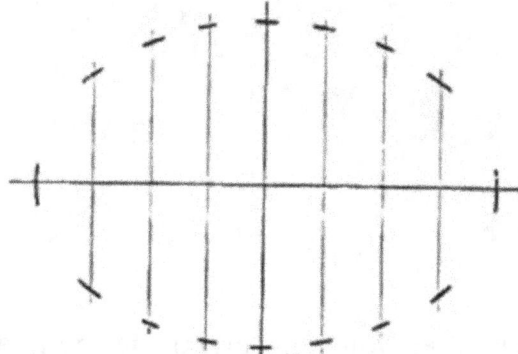

Rule vertical lines from left to right, the same distance apart, and add a little extra length to each line as you approach the main center vertical line.

Make as many lines as you like but have at least as many as shown in the diagram above and ensure that they diminish gradually in length both to the right and left of the main vertical center line.

Now mark off the respective lengths and draw a curve through those marks to obtain an ellipse. Notice in the example that the marks are slanted except for the original 2 crossed lines which have straight marks.

While this method is not practical for freehand drawing, it is an excellent way to learn how to create an ellipse. You can now easily distinguish whether the shape of a flower (for example) is circular or at an angle where the elliptical shape is required.

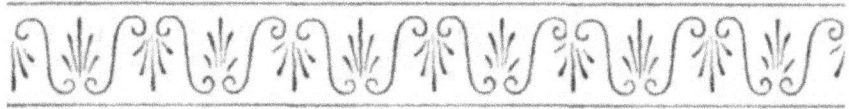

05 - USING YOUR NEW SKILLS

EXERCISE FOUR

To successfully sketch nature, you need to know how to portray the parts that make a whole so take a few moments to collect a few leaves and twigs to practice with.

It's good to do some stimulating exercises to get your hand/eye co-ordination working and in form. As usual, it's best to start simple and luckily there are basic leaves which have charming curves, as in Figure 10.

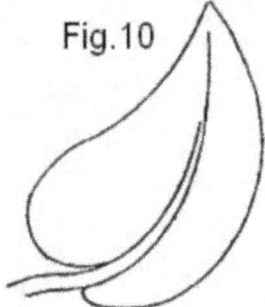

Fig.10

Do you remember when you were practicing the lines within a square boundary and you learned to look ahead to the destination dots? Well, here is where you use that skill because you need to look ahead to finish the second half of the leaf at the appropriate spot.

A good habit for right-handers is to start on the left side of all drawings and vice versa for left-handers.

Now try a wavy edge like this one in Figure 11...

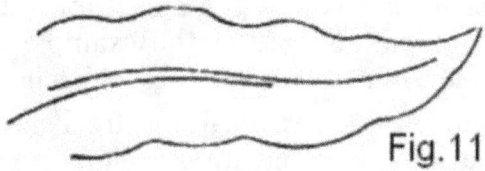

Fig.11

The original reference picture needs to be examined each and every time you practice it - you don't get the real benefits of 'learning to see' when copying from your own work.

It does help to visualize the end result you want and transmit that thought to your pencil.

Figure 12 shows a natural fold in a leaf...

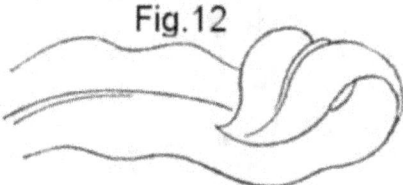

Observe the width of the leaf and the position of the folded tip as you practice copying it over and over again.

The arrow below shows how far the folded part is from the edge of the leaf - these are the types of observations you need to make when copying.

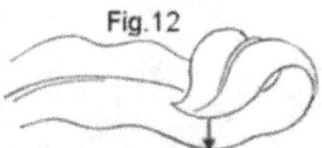

The shaded portion below shows the shape of an area that you can use or refer to when comparing your illustration with the original. You might find it easier to draw this shape, rather than focusing solely on outline.

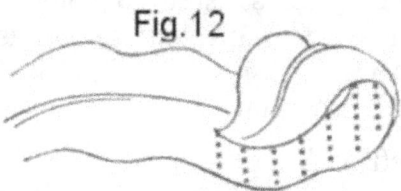

I know it seems like there is a lot to remember but observation is very important and you only have to make it a habit to save any strain on your memory.

You will develop your own way of producing different subjects but if you are unsure how to approach the creation of Figure 12, here is the step by step process that I was comfortable with:

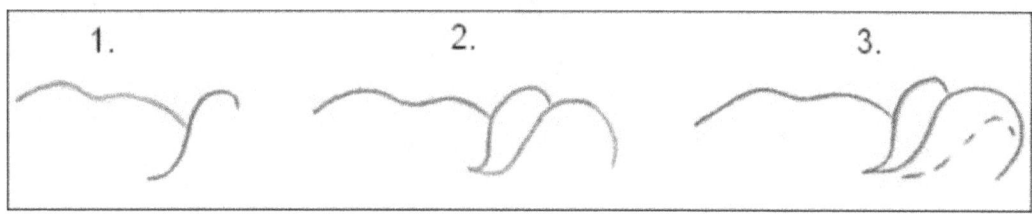

In the following Figure 13, you don't have to mimic every variation in the outline - simply try to achieve something that looks similar. When you sketch from nature, you aren't really going to illustrate all of these fussy little bits. This exercise is simply to get your hand in tune with nature.

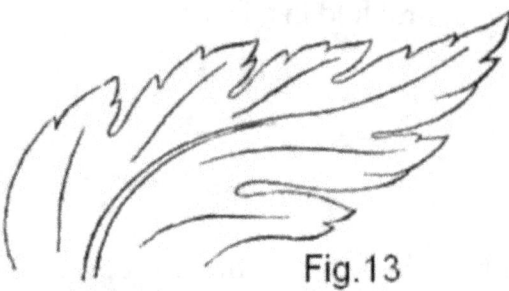

Fig.13

As you study this leaf, notice how every division in the leaf points in the direction of growth. This is how you give a sense of life to your sketches, by including indicators of flow and direction.

Prior to starting practice on Fig.13, visualize the shape you want to portray and it'll work out, don't just focus on copying the lines.

Be bold, experiment with different ways to create the leaf above and you ultimately decide which approach suits you best. I had the most success with drawing the stem first and building the leaf around that line.

The best thing you can do is listen to your instinct, what you feel comfortable with and how you want your drawings to appear. Your own true style will evolve naturally - it is there from the beginning but it's up to you to nurture it to its full potential.

Once you've practiced and are satisfied with results, you are well on your way to producing good illustrations. It's all about building up your confidence and knowing in advance that you can draw whatever you like!

The next practice session is to do with observing and drawing stems. For general knowledge purposes, note that most stems diminish in length and thickness as they extend. This is an easy exercise so put your brain in neutral and just enjoy it.

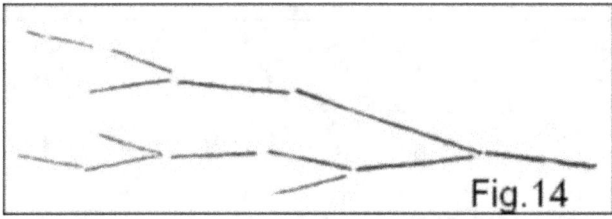

Fig.14

Instead of drawing parallel lines to denote the thickness of a twig, you can simply press harder on the pencil and then lighten the stroke as it makes its way outward to the tips. Finding shortcuts is my most favorite thing!

Tendrils also play a part in nature and the best examples are seen on vines or honeysuckles. They are generally depicted in the form of spirals, as shown in Figure 15.

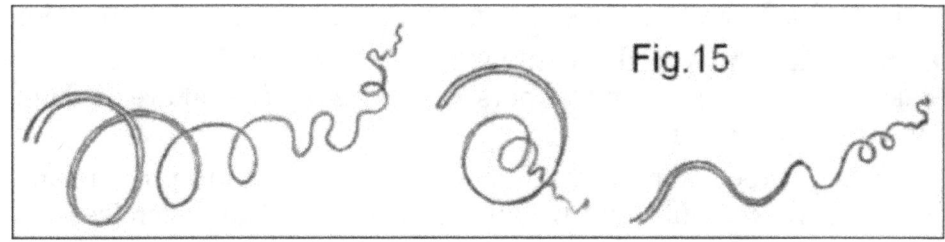

Fig.15

We have already practiced drawing plain spirals so now it's time to implement that skill while drawing these items from Nature.

Buds make a delightful drawing topic. Any practice is good practice, so keep going, you're doing great!

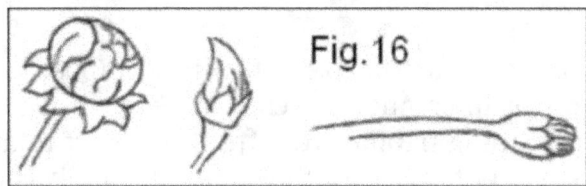

Fig.16

Loops and folds in leaves are nearly always in conjunction with one another. If you take a piece of paper and make folds in it (see Figure 17), look at it angle wise to see the folds forming the appearance of loops.

The sides of the folds (running vertically) can only be represented by straight or curved lines and these lines start from each end of the loops.

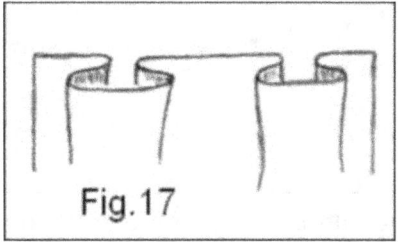

Fig.17

So when you have a folded leaf, you depict it the same way, as in Fig 18.

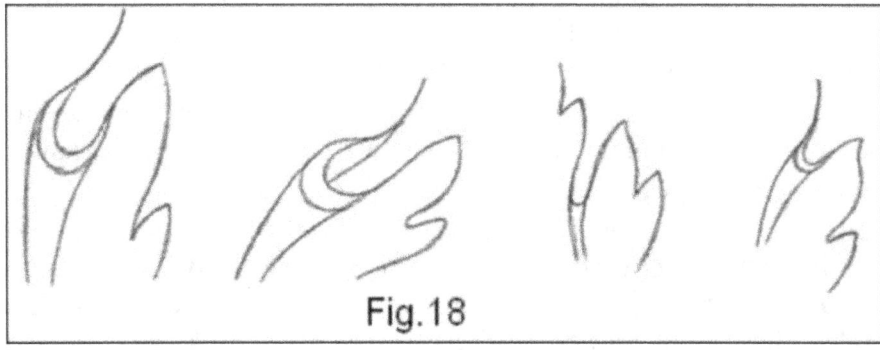

Fig.18

Don't just look at these illustrations, make a point to draw them so you are familiar with them before you sketch outdoors.

Observation is the key for every artist. When you are confident that you are actually drawing what you see, you won't really need any instruction.

Observation helps you draw things in their proper size and location so that takes care of proportion and perspective - 2 topics that are difficult for beginner artists to grasp.

I know I'd rather learn to rely on my eyes than study proportion and perspective, what about you? If you seriously do all the exercises in this book, you zoom to the top faster than those who are in college studying the theory of it all.

These simple exercises not only assist hand/eye co-ordination, they are teaching you to observe the way an artist does. That means we have to erase our own ideas of what things look like and stay true to the topic we want to portray.

The next exercise is to familiarize you with Composition of Line which is the arrangement of lines and curves that need to lead in a particular direction and not jumping haphazardly from one part to another. When a leaf is crossing a stem, both parts of the stem must look as if they belong to one another, and should be in the same line or curve of growth, as in the first drawing in Figure 19.

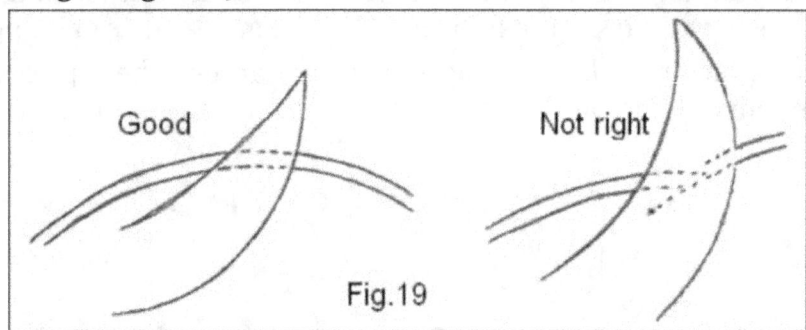

In the drawing on the right, the two parts of the stem do not appear in the same line of growth.

To get the correct effect, you may prefer to draw the stem continuous at first, then the leaf across it (or vice versa), and afterwards erase the parts of stem or leaf not wanted, as shown by the dotted lines above.

I find drawing an imaginary line across the leaf (raising the pencil just a fraction above the paper) keeps the correct flow and it's easier than inserting and erasing.

If you are right-handed, draw the curve on the left first. If you do the right curve first, it's covered by the hand and you have no reference or guide. Do the reverse if you are left-handed. Don't hesitate to turn the paper if that helps you get firm and even curves.

06 - CLUMPS AND CLUSTERS

EXERCISE FIVE

The foliage of trees is made up of irregular curved lines that form into semicircles, angles, or points, according to the character of the tree. These forms go in all directions so you need to learn how to express them in whichever way they appear to the eye.

Starting with semicircle-type foliage, copy the first image below (from left to right) several times. Once you become familiar with the first one, move on to creating the clusters.

Remember, there's no need to imitate every stroke exactly, just try to capture something similar in your own style. Visualize your strokes all going towards the center where leaves meet twigs.

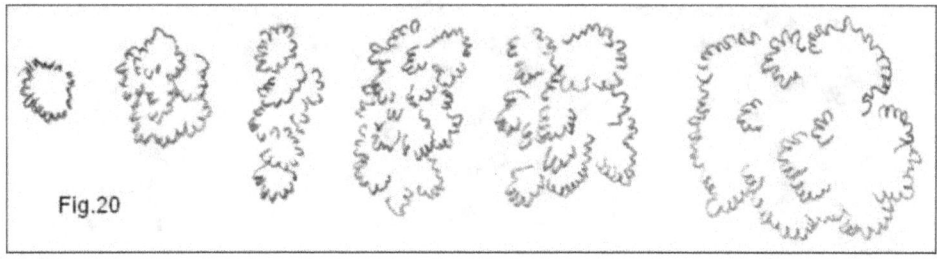

Fig.20

Do you see how some clusters look like fingers? Sometimes it helps the illustration process when you make comparisons to things you are very familiar with.

Now try practicing with pointed foliage, start on the left and progress onto the next example once you feel ready.

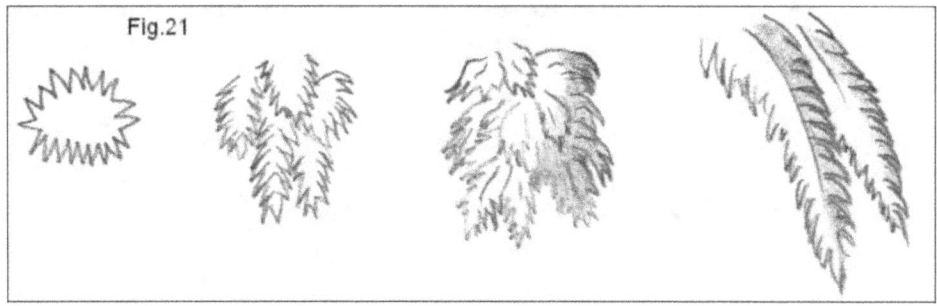

Fig.21

I used a 7B pencil to draw and shade the 3rd and 4th illustrations - it's a very soft and dark graphite.

The next unusual looking specimen, figure 22, is familiar to Oak trees and it's different to most.

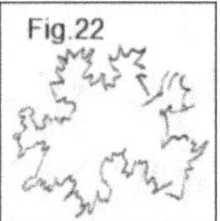

Definitely do not try to copy it exactly, just aim for the general look. Drawing is meant to be a peaceful pastime so don't allow little things to frustrate you. With every single attempt you will improve.

It is fun reproducing these weird shapes because you get to interpret what you see within them and that adds a bit of entertainment to an ordinary practice session. I thought my version above looked like a cat that had received a terrible fright - do you see that, too? In the shaded similar shape below, I see a dog walking on hind legs with a full knapsack on his back!

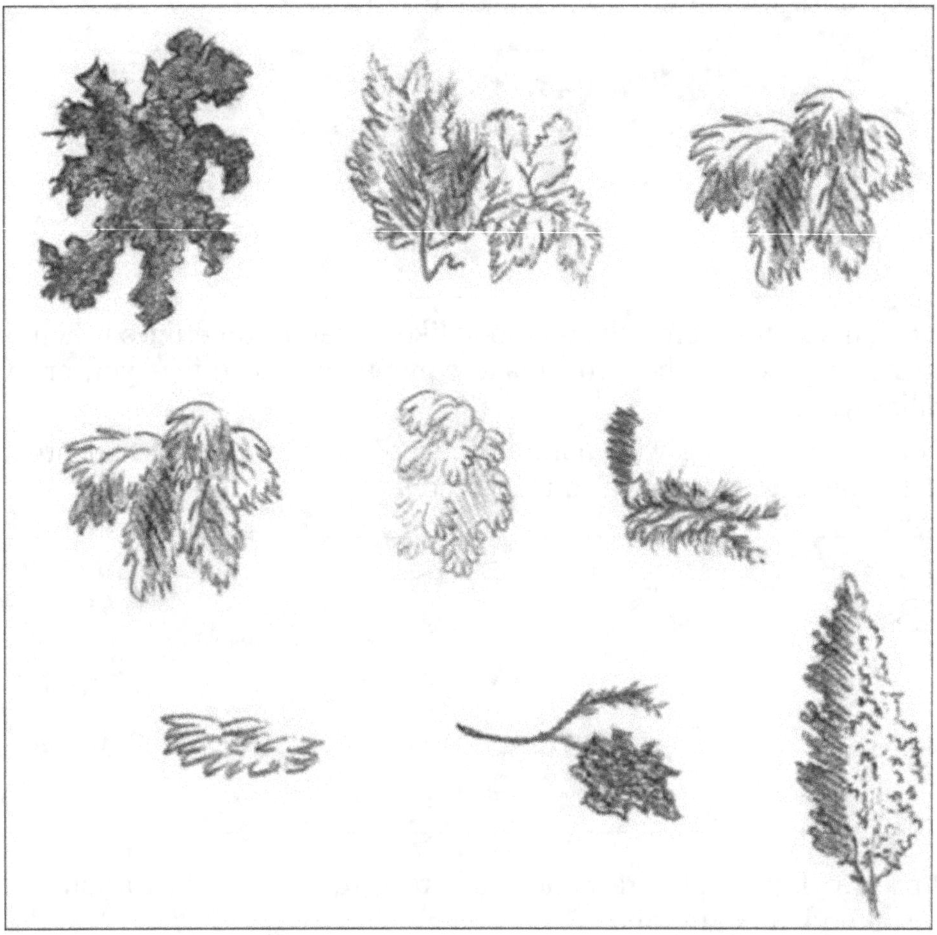

07 - BASIC LIGHT AND SHADE TIP

EXERCISE SIX

Light and Shade is a really big topic which could form a book of its own but it helps to be armed with basic knowledge so you can start sketching from nature as soon as possible. We all learn by practicing and, in my opinion, gradual learning is the best process. Can you imagine waiting until you know everything there is to know before you start? Goodness, we'd never get to draw!

So, when you want to portray bright light or reflection in a sketch, make the surrounding area comparatively darker.

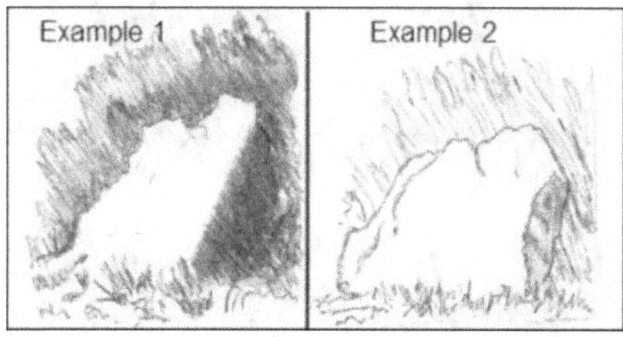

In the examples here, the light on the stone in example 1 appears brighter or stronger than it does on the stone in example 2. This is because the first stone is relieved by a darker toned mass of shade.

The simplest form of effect is the opposition of two masses. If a subject is dark, as in a building or a group of trees, it can be relieved by a light sky; if buildings or trees are light, make the sky darker.

Some of the most charming effects in nature are those resulting from the direct opposition of light and dark.

So when you think your sketch is lacking something, tinker with adding some shade.

There is so much to learn about light and shade but this single tip is enough for all beginners to give their drawings a bit of sparkle.

08 - IMAGES TO COPY

Select any of the following images that appeal to you and copy them as many times as you like.

With each one your drawing and observation skills improve. It really is the best way to enjoy any practice session. Be proud of your achievements!

These are the same images I used for practice...

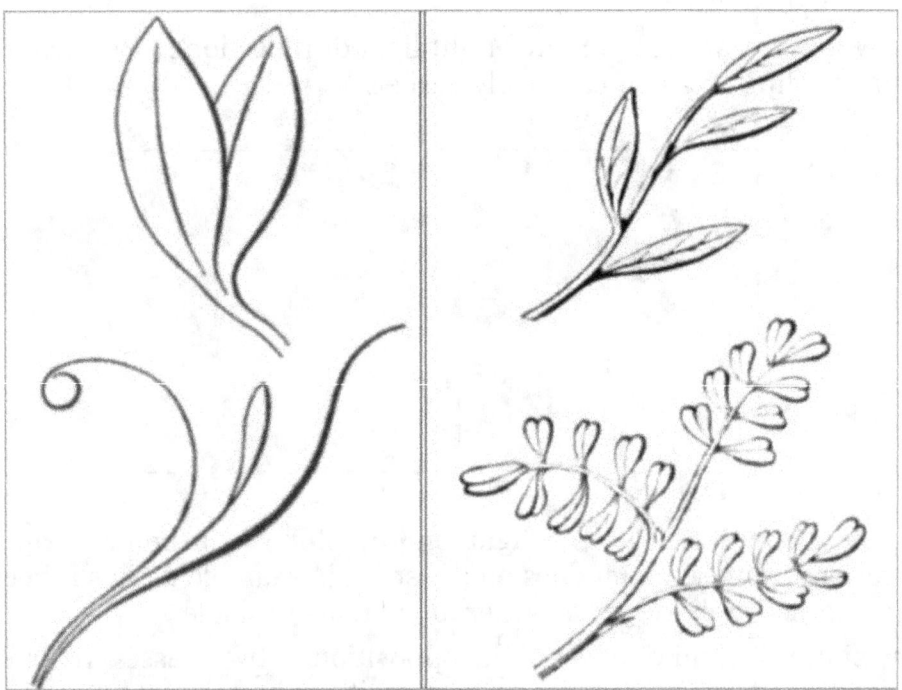

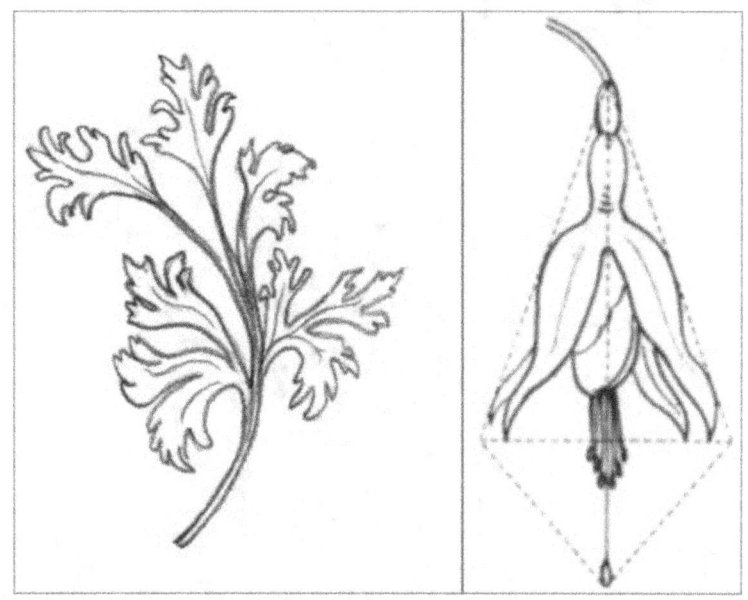

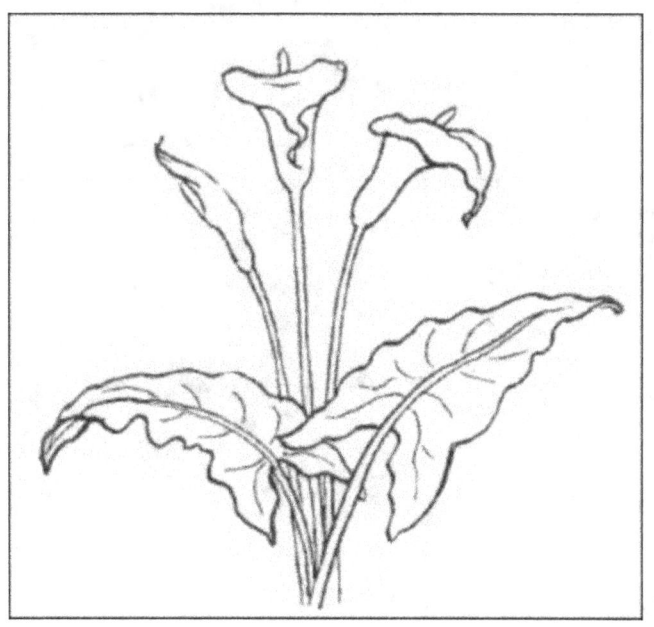

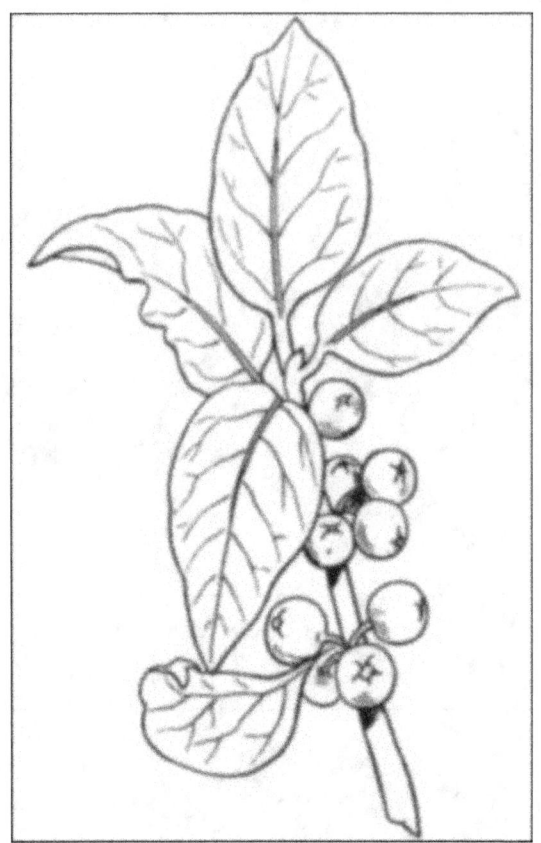

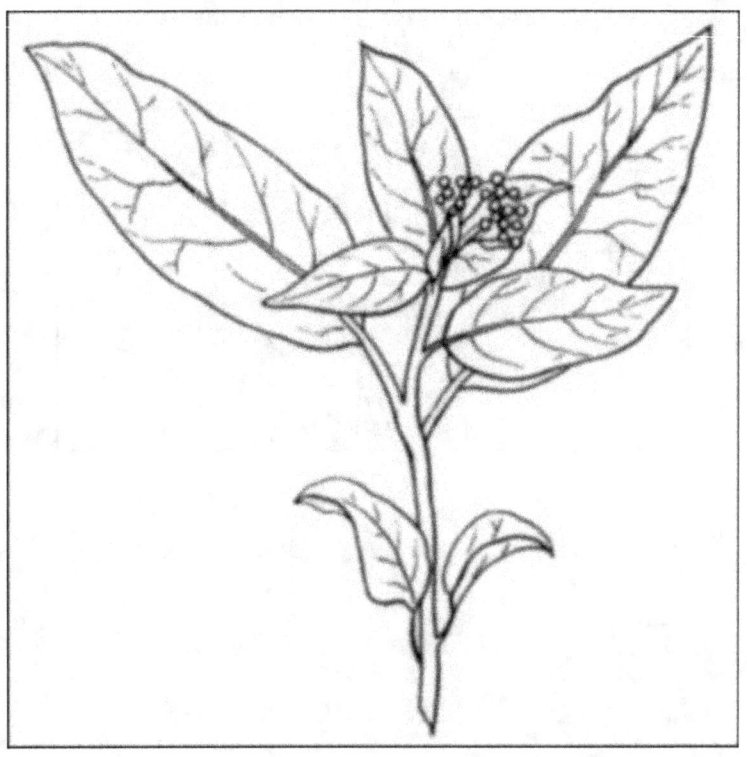

09 - HOW TO DRAW OUTLINES – BOOK 2

INTRODUCTION

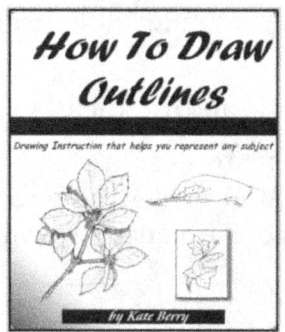

There are many different ways to get an image down on paper so these tips are based on the easiest and most successful methods I discovered while teaching myself to draw.

Once you know how to draw, you have another language at your disposal that you can use to express your thoughts.

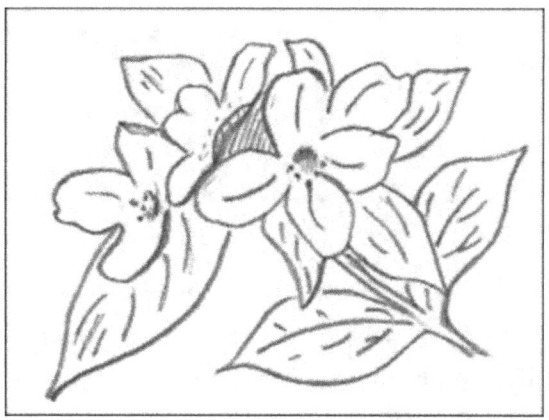

You do have creative ability and by copying the wonderful selection of outlines in this book and using the tips provided, you will surely find it.

It's all a matter of progression... start with a basic outline and eventually, over time, you find yourself completing interesting drawings without any boring study! That's why I compiled this book -- to show you the easiest way to get that starting outline down on paper.

The trick is to learn in stages, to practice one thing until you are comfortable and then move on.

Grids are a terrific drawing aid but they are no good if you want to draw outdoors. The options laid out here show you how to draw anywhere and at any time without being dependent on grids.

In the following drawings, I mostly used a 2B, 3B or 5B wood pencil and for very fine line work (as in the plant stems) I used a 2B mechanical pencil. Hold your pencil in a comfortable grip to speed up the learning process.

Best erasers -- white plastic and/or kneaded.

Drawing supplies and materials are not discussed in great detail because this book is dedicated to showing you how to achieve a simple outline that forms the basis of a finished drawing.

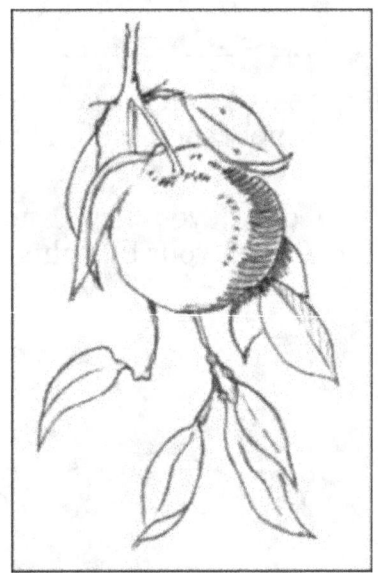

There are 9 methods (or options) in this section to help you draw outlines successfully. Each method is shown with examples so you can select what suits you the best.

Well, no time for idle chatter, let's get started!

10 - BLOCKING-IN

METHOD ONE

Blocking-in lines are sketched lines limiting an object or group of objects to a definite field.

Artists "block in" (or sketch with light lines) the general proportion and shape of objects by using straight lines. This enables you to make several adjustments prior to drawing the final line and this is how to avoid errors.

The best way to draw successfully the first time is to sketch very simply or block-in lines that indicate the size, shape and position of parts, before spending any time on technique or careful drawing.

Fig. 1 shows a typical example of what happens when we draw without guidelines.

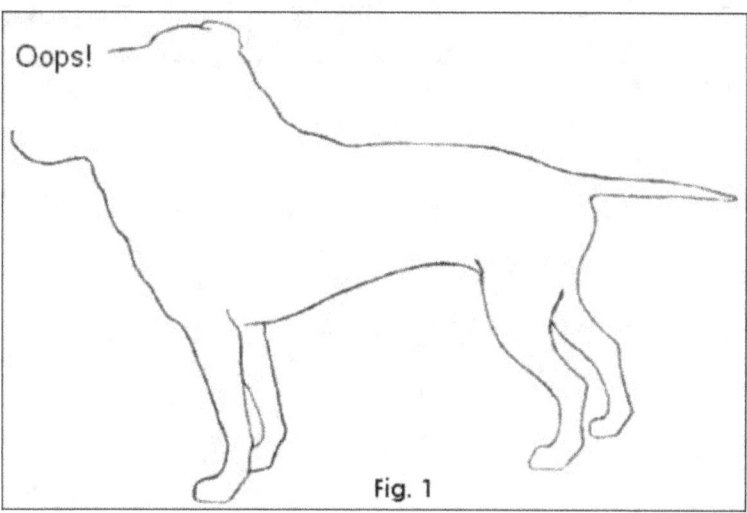

Oops!

Fig. 1

If I begin with the nose first and continue the line of the head, back etc., I am focused on the line rather than the general proportion and it finishes up distorted. A lot of my drawings turned out just like this until I discovered the block-in method.

Prior to blocking-in and prior to commencing any drawing, it helps to estimate the height and width of the subject and make the appropriate marks on paper.

If you don't like to draw within a border, you may prefer to simply draw a base line along the bottom to help keep the drawing level.

Fig. 2 below shows a better way to begin. Sketch in these guidelines lightly. (They are made darker here for your viewing.)

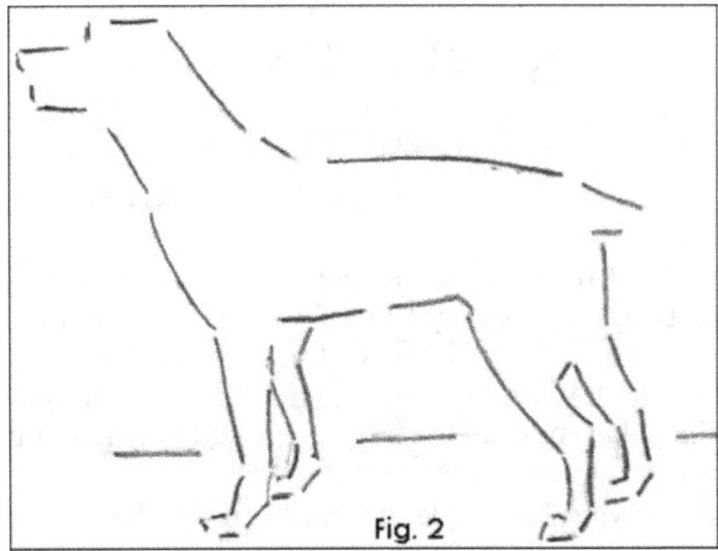

Fig. 2

Fig. 3 shows the result after using the lighter block lines as a guide.

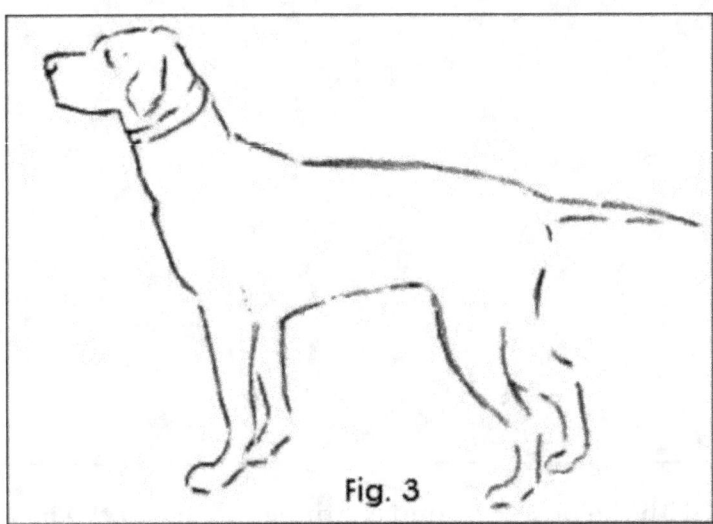

Fig. 3

Hold your pencil loosely and try to feel the form as you fill it in with a series of light lines. Without erasing, change and redraw the sketchy lines until you find the right line. You save a lot of time by keeping the incorrect lines because that ensures you don't repeat them.

When you are satisfied with the outline, make the correct lines a little darker than the others and then you can erase the lighter ones.

Copying drawings is a form of art study. It helps to provide a regular sequence to art students along with good examples of form, line and composition. Treat it as an intermediate stage while learning to draw.

It took me a while to realize that drawing fruit is a great way to learn about perspective (without intensive theory study) and how to arrange objects before you draw them.

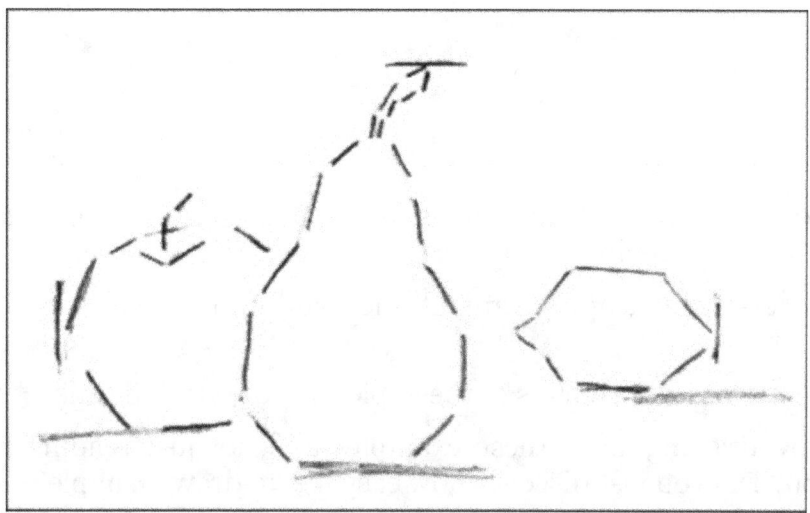

Start off by indicating the height and width of the group with a light pencil touch and then lightly block in the various items in the group to keep the right proportions.

The effect of distance is obtained by placing the lemon higher up (on the paper) than the pear and apple, and make it smaller with lighter lines. This is a great tip to remember!

When you study an apple, you note the difference between the height and width and draw to those proportions.

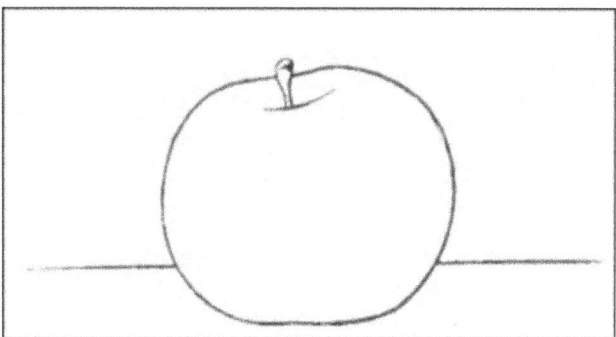

The general shape is circular but it is not a perfect circle.

Say the apple is wider than it is high so make some marks on your paper to those rough dimensions (see following Fig 1).

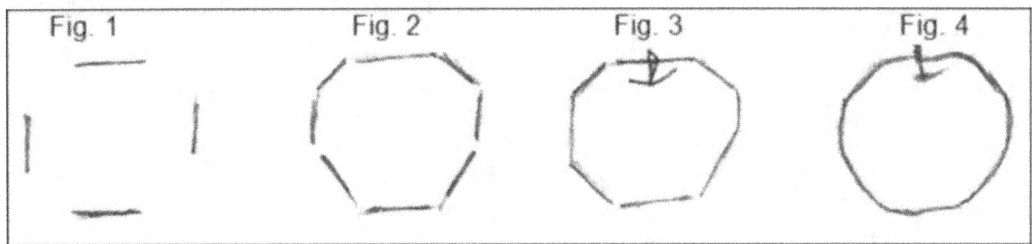

Figure 2 -- draw all straight lines, indicating the round shoulders with slanted lines but keeping them straight.

Figure 3 -- again keeping straight lines, add in the stem and the hollow where it sits.

Figure 4 -- draw the curves of the apple over the straight lines.

You *are* drawing all of these examples and not just reading about it, aren't you? Did you just discover how easy it is to draw an apple?

Apply this format to anything circular that you wish to draw. Don't forget to estimate the height versus width and you will achieve a good likeness.

Below you see the stages for drawing a leaf. In Figure 1, the shape is blocked-in and in Fig. 2, the veins are added in straight lines.

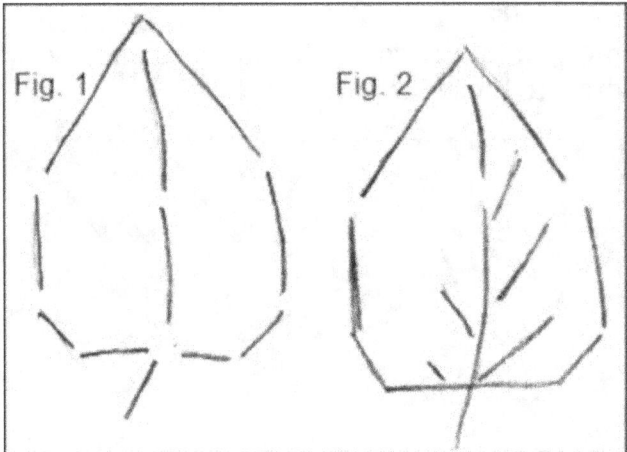

In Figure 3, the curves are drawn and in Figure 4, the leaf is completed. (Remember that normally the block in lines are ultra-light.)

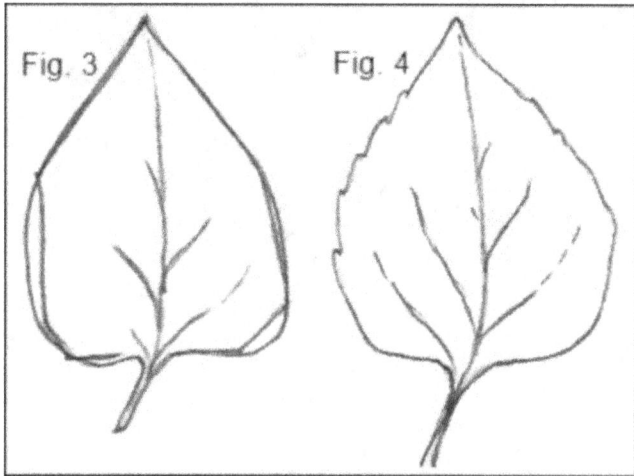

Let's do a study to imprint the process in our minds -- start off by putting a real leaf on some drawing paper.

Now proceed to...

* Block around it with straight lines.

* Remove the leaf from your paper.

* Draw the leaf stalk and a few veins within the block lines.

* Draw over the lines with more suitable strokes and erase guidelines.

* Finish the leaf with soft lines. Adjust the pressure on your pencil to vary the width of lines and add some effect.

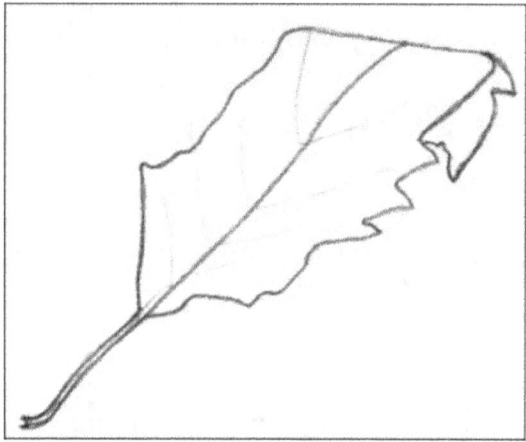

This straightforward exercise builds your confidence when you see such immediate and successful results.

Blocking-in shows the general proportion and direction by the use of straight lines. Pay no attention to details because this is simply a quick way of showing the general outline.

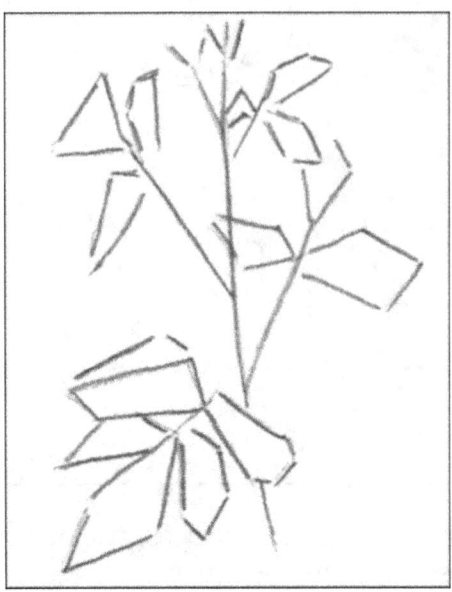

The rough example above shows how I blocked in my drawing (below) of leaves on a branch.

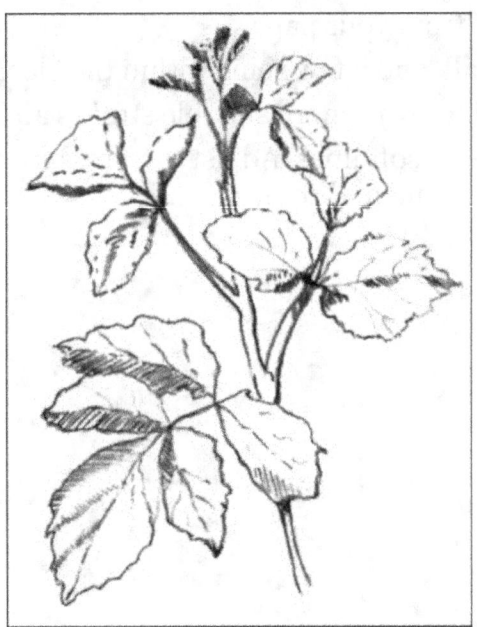

Blocking-in the outline saves any confusion you might first experience when looking at plants to draw. Never try to copy Nature exactly as it is, just <u>observe the direction of the main stem</u> and select a few of the secondary stems that you want to include.

Each subject may require a different approach for the initial blocking in. For example, when I draw an animal, I like to use a larger shape like a rectangle or oval for the body and I build my smaller block-in lines from that anchor point.

Of course, if you wish, you can use all sorts of shapes to make up the whole form -- like circles, squares, cylinders and so on. However, I found the following method the easiest way for me to draw animals.

This next exercise is based around a reference picture of a wolf drinking water from a stream.

First I draw a rough base line as a starting point. Using that line as a guide, I draw in the slope of the ground where the wolf was standing. Those 2 lines help get the drawing started and they are then used to constantly compare and gauge angles.

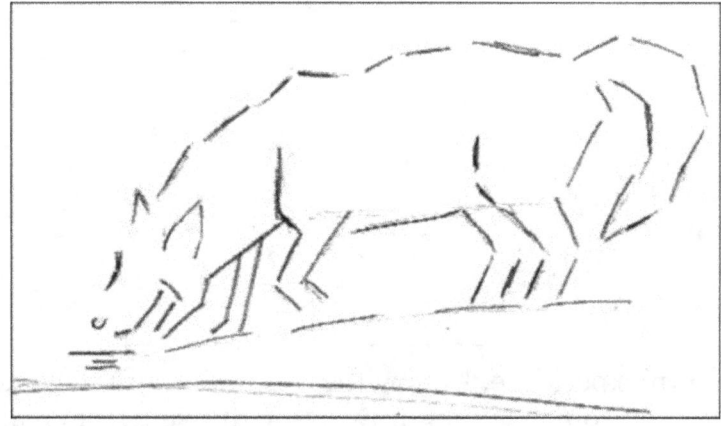

I estimate the angle and distance of the wolf's tummy from the ground prior to sketching the largest piece (i.e. the rectangle) which represents the body of the wolf.

In the image above, you might be able to see a light line that I initially used as part of the rectangle but it was incorrect so I drew in another, placing it more in line with the angle of the ground.

Once you have the image blocked in, you can see if it is right to proceed and finish off the drawing, as shown below.

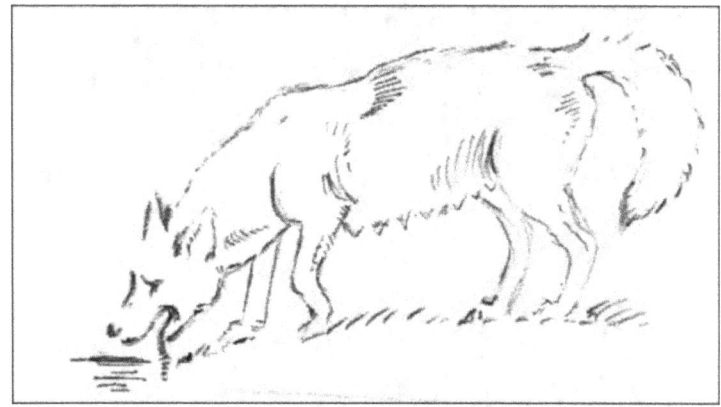

Dab at the unwanted lines with a kneaded eraser (molded to a point), so it won't upset any of the lines you want to keep.

Here's a duck which has been blocked in, ready for you to finish off.

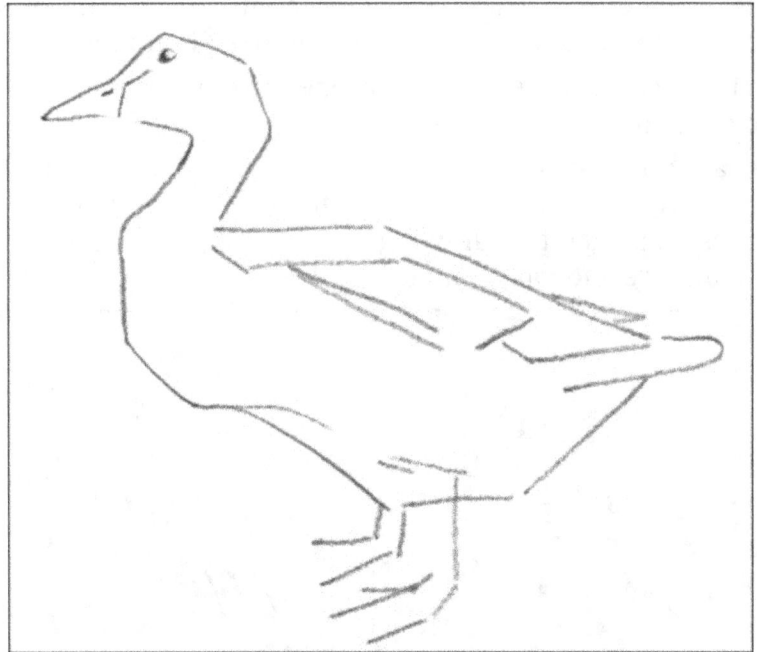

From my own experience, I know there is a kind of reluctance to make the transition from copying other drawings to drawing from real life.

Just adopt and utilize one of the methods explained here that you feel most comfortable with and make yourself do it. You'll make mistakes but remember everyone else does, too! The thing is, it's a progressive step in the right direction and you won't look back.

Draw step by step with me...

Let me take you through the process of drawing an azalea picked from my garden (pictured here).

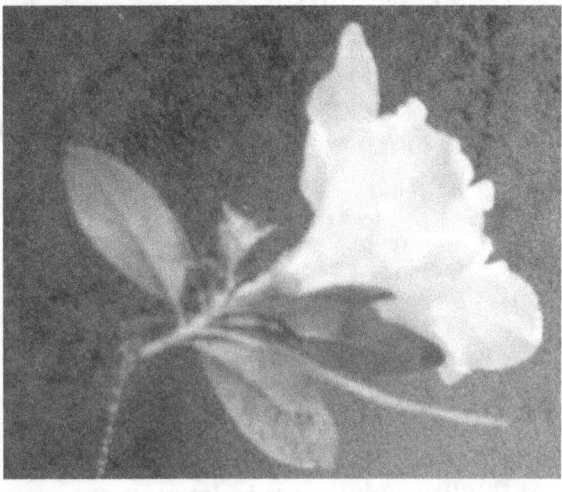

I chose to use the block-in method along with the simplest view of the flower which is side-on. The following drawing is done from real life and not the photo.

A 2B mechanical pencil was used for the initial blocking-in as well as for most of the finished drawing, except when I used a 3B to hide a lot of the lighter, uncertain lines (instead of using an eraser).

1. First up, I drew the main stem and then the only secondary stem that is growing from there, as you can see in the following example (the lines are darkened for display purposes).

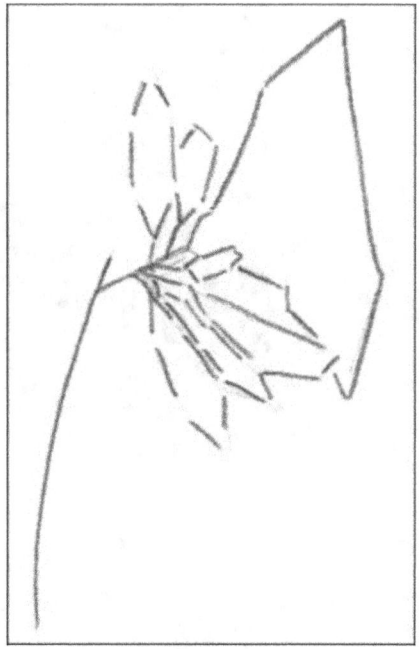

2. Add the block-in leaves along the secondary stem. It definitely helps to convert all curves to straight lines because the image appears quickly, showing the potential of a good outcome.

3. Block in the flower - study the shape of the flower and design a similar overall shape.

4. Do a quick comparison of the flower with the block-lines to ensure you have captured the general outline.

5. It's time to start filling out the drawing, let the fun begin!

Go over the 'good' lines with more pressure before you erase the lighter, incorrect lines with a gentle swipe of a kneaded eraser. (I am repeating myself in case you missed that tip first time around!)

6. To achieve a steady thin stem, put a series of dots close to the original or main line and join them up, using the dot-to-dot system as mentioned in Method # 7 and as seen in the drawing over page.

The dots fit in well with the texture of the real stem so you don't have to bother with erasing them later.

7. Progress along the secondary stem and draw over your block lines to complete each leafs appearance.

8. Notice and record how the flower is attached to the stem and proceed onto completing the outline of the flower to its true shape.

I wanted a simplistic drawing so I only added stippling (dots) to the leaves and made some marks on the petals to portray the position of veins.

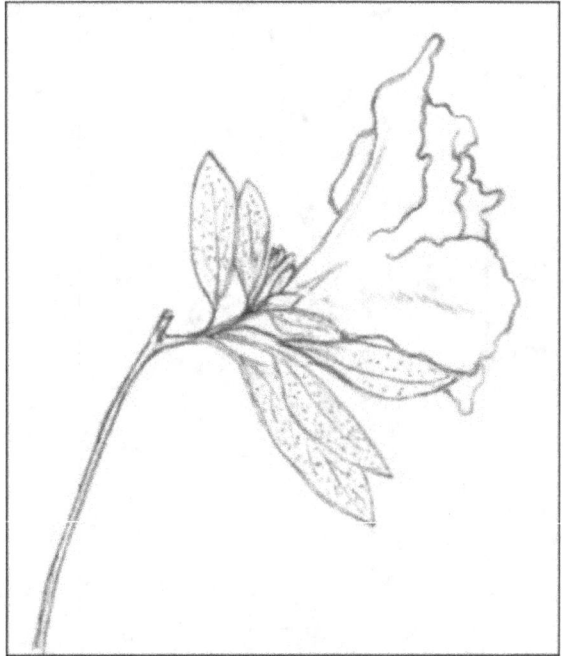

So, that's how you go from copying drawings at home and moving on to real life!

Most examples in this book are drawn from Nature because it is such a flexible topic, it sees new artists progress from wobbly lines to confident and sure lines.

In the meantime, your artwork can't be criticized because no one can say if your drawing is true or not and that allows your confidence to grow without any hiccups along the way.

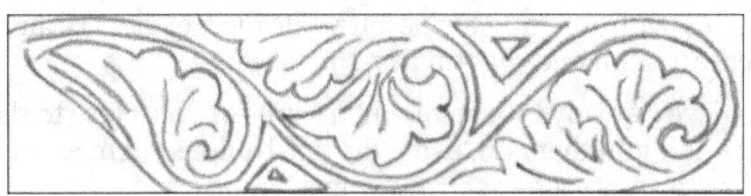

11 - VISUALIZING A BROADER OUTLINE

METHOD TWO

There is also an option to block-in using no particular shape, just go around the outline roughly using straight lines only.

If you copy from a picture in a magazine, draw lines around the image and copy that similar shape onto your paper. This kind of practice enables you to visualize the block (or border) when you are outdoors, giving you something to build upon.

Once you have the odd shape roughed out, proceed to make the line variations or indents necessary to create an image within those guidelines.

This is a perfect method when you can't see familiar shapes within a chosen subject.

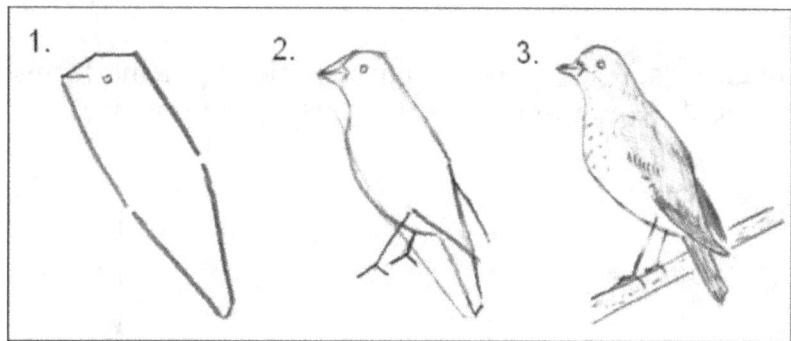

Trust your senses to draw an outline that you can proceed to develop.

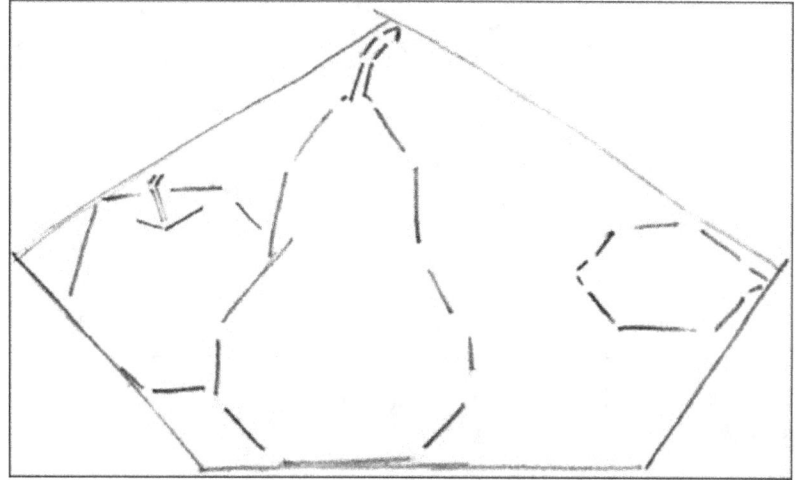

To refine this method further, see the bird outline below that consists of an oval, straight lines and a couple of curves.

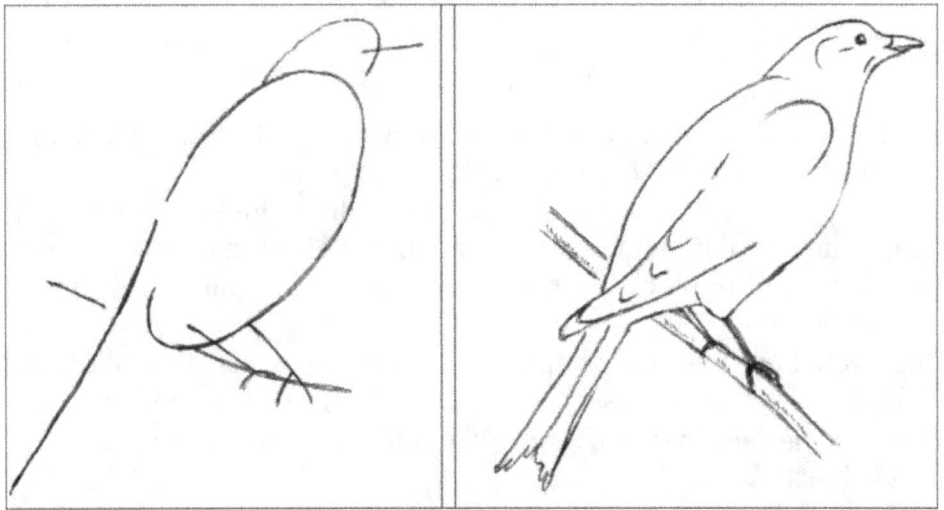

Go through magazines or books and practice reducing forms to these types of simple strokes. You won't regret this type of practice!

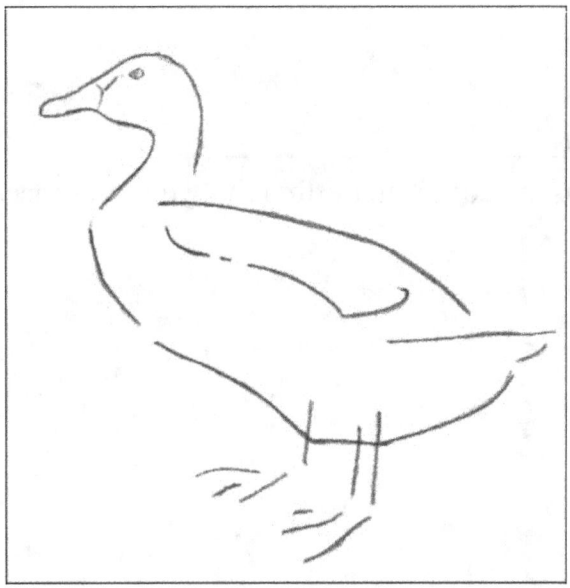

12 - RECOGNIZING SHAPES

METHOD THREE

If you are not comfortable with blocking in, experiment with another option like trying to visualize what shapes you see while looking at the object you want to draw.

Some flowers represent familiar objects and again, this helps us to understand the form of the flowers better.

For example, some might say the Morning Glory flower looks like a funnel, rather than a circle on top of a cylinder.

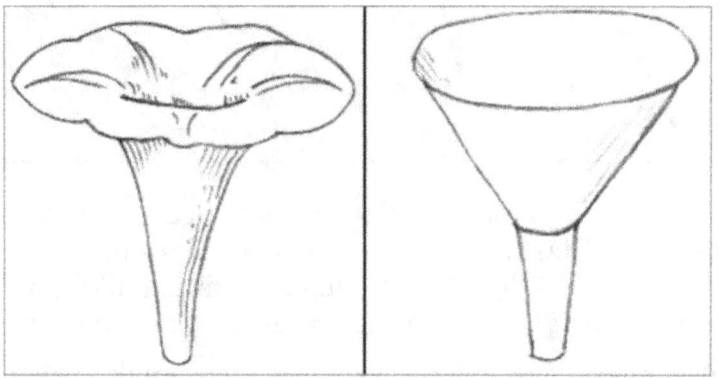

Comparing your chosen subject with something familiar makes it easier to visualize and sketch.

It doesn't matter which shapes you choose, use whatever you see because it usually differs for each of us. Simplify the shapes to whatever you like.

This isn't a system I use but it does work for some people and that's why I'm including it.

When you're learning to draw, it's a good idea to establish a rhythm by finding the best way to get an outline on paper and to feel the flow of the pencil beneath your fingers.

Once you've made some marks, the blank page syndrome vanishes and everything is easier from that point onwards.

For the flower below, rather than block in each petal, it can be created from a simple square and some other helpful guidelines.

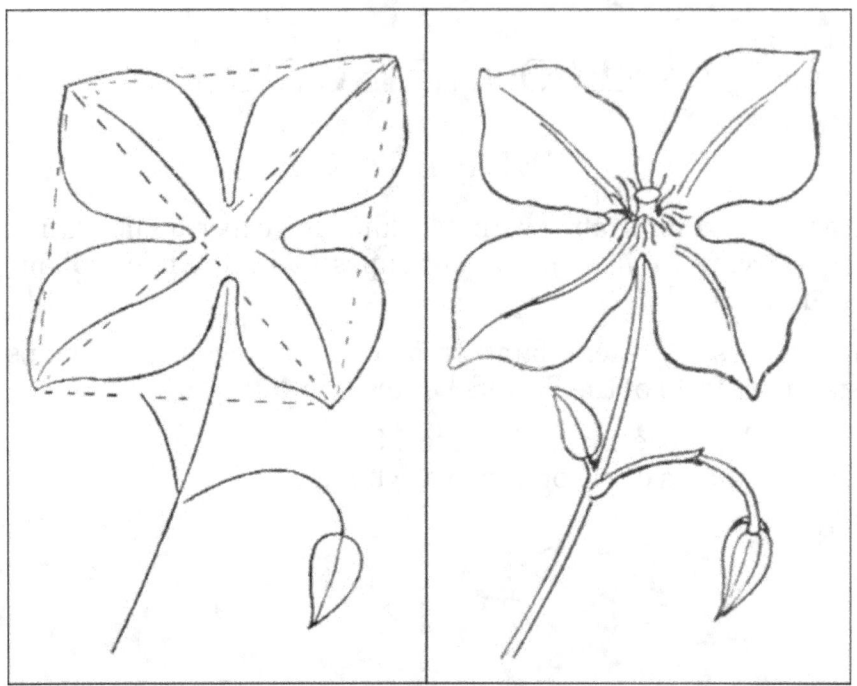

Even though you only have basic shapes appearing on paper, you are now in a position to start adding more detailed lines to bring the drawing to life. These lines are all lightly sketched in and that allows you to change it as you become more aware of the appearance of each portion.

Sometimes internal guidelines can be intentionally left in for extra effect. As the artist, you are the architect and the finished design is an original by you!

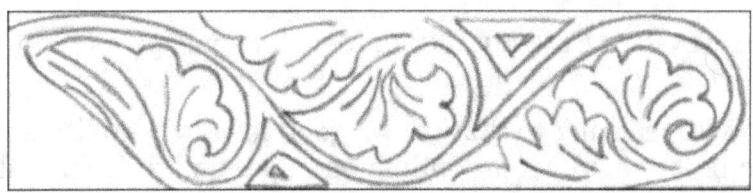

13 - IDENTIFYING LETTERS

METHOD FOUR

As previously discussed, a useful trick for artists is to study a subject and convert it into a common form. To vary that a little, let's look for letters of the alphabet.

For example, notice how a butterfly can resemble the letter X...

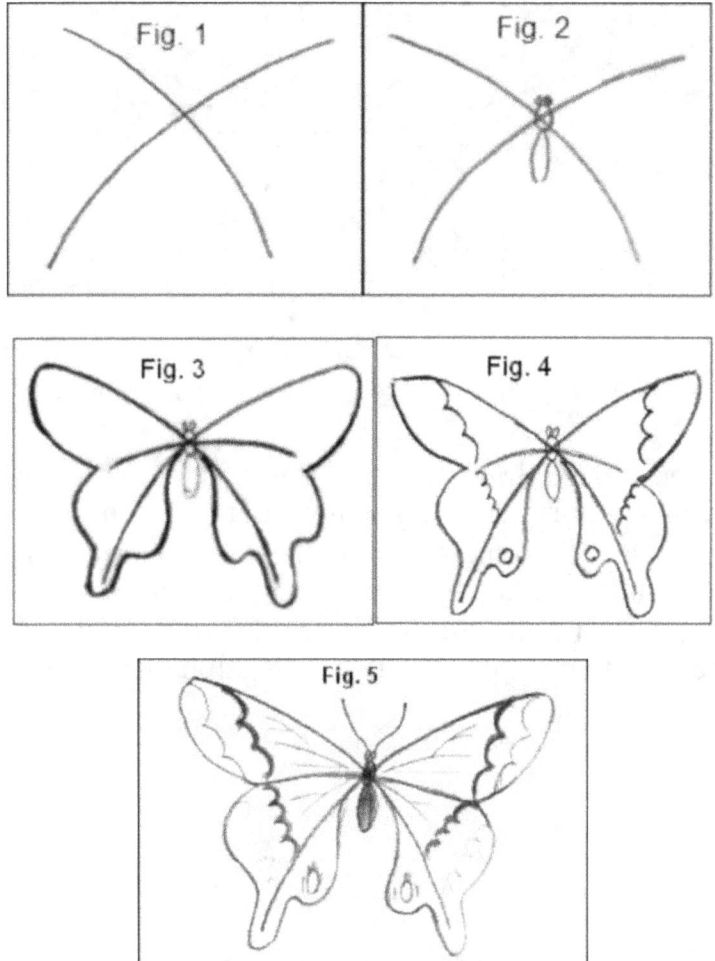

Once you practice these progressive steps, you will move onto creating some really interesting pieces from your imagination.

Here is another butterfly, only this time with the letter Y...

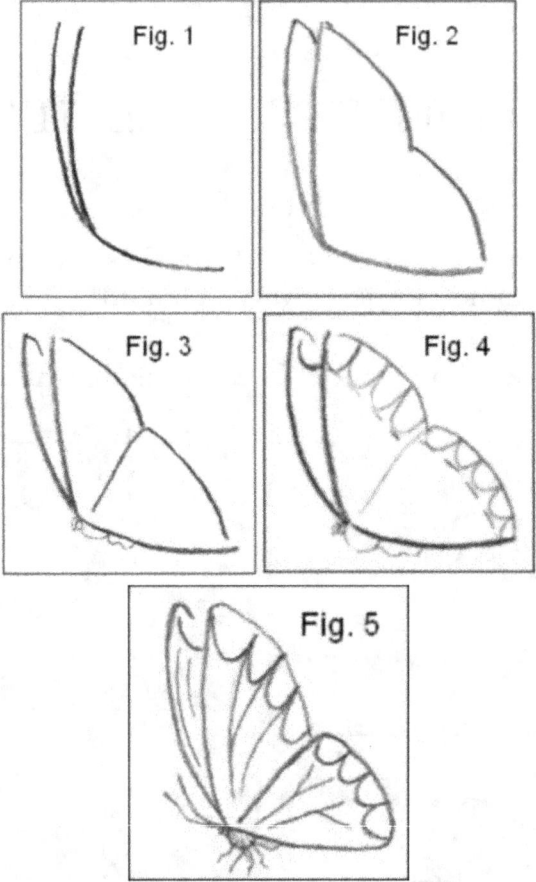

Do these step by step drawings a few times and you'll always be able to draw them from memory. That is the power of repetition!

The connection with something familiar helps you to quickly get the drawing started and it's something you won't ever forget.

This is why I can't believe it when people say "I don't know what to draw". All we have to do is pick a letter of the alphabet and start inventing our drawings!

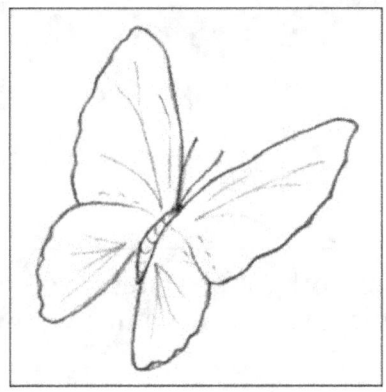

14 - CONSTRUCTION DRAWINGS

METHOD FIVE

Construction deals with the form of objects and it is an important tool for creating a truthful drawing.

A mouse has the simple form of a semi-circle but it is really the tail that gives the impression of a mouse.

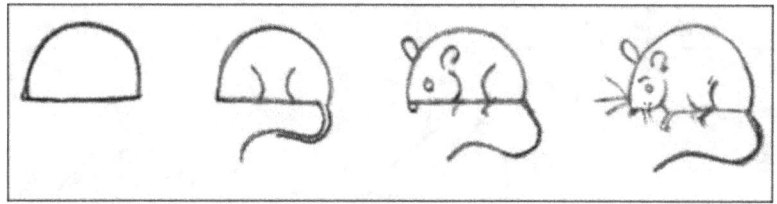

The rear view of a mouse can be converted into a series of circles...

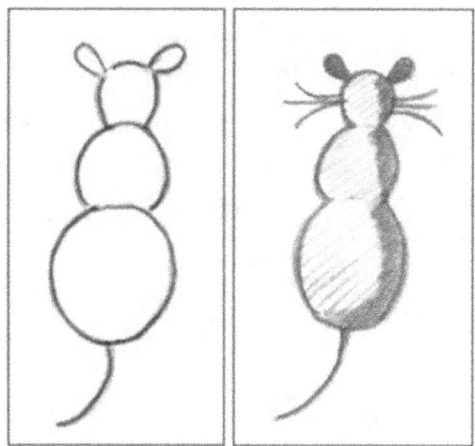

Due to the repetitive nature of step by step drawing, the images become imprinted in your mind and that enables easy recall later on.

Let's construct a fish the easy way...

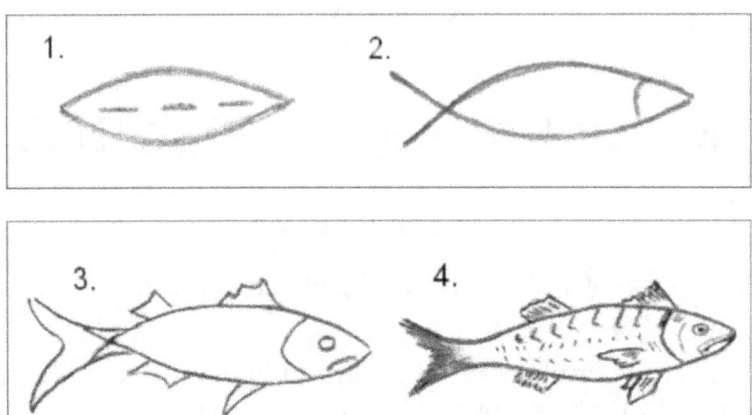

How to visualize and draw cherries...

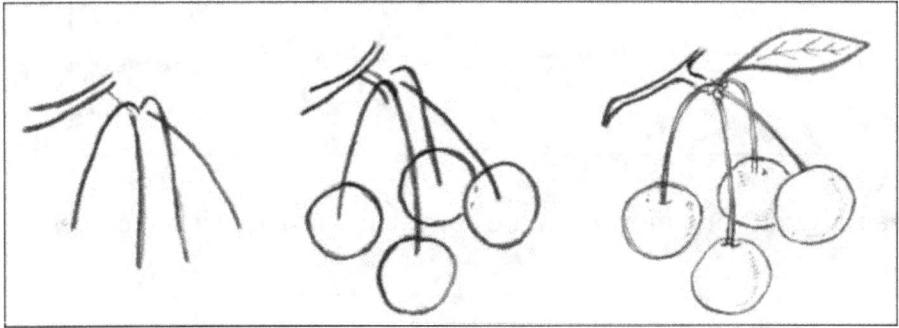

5 Simple steps to create most flowers...

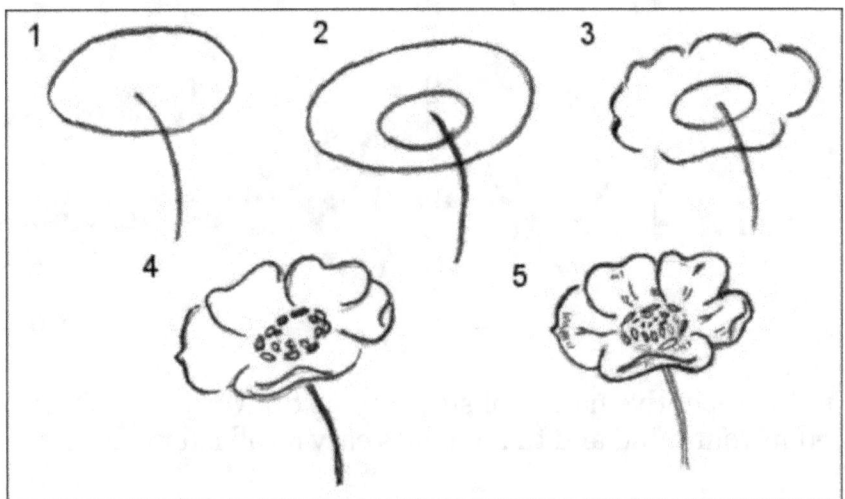

The drawing methods you see here are working drawings -- you won't always use these methods but it's a fantastic way to lead you into creating future drawings.

You become more aware of the relation of parts to a subject and this knowledge contributes towards your creative imagination. See the 5 steps to drawing a bee...

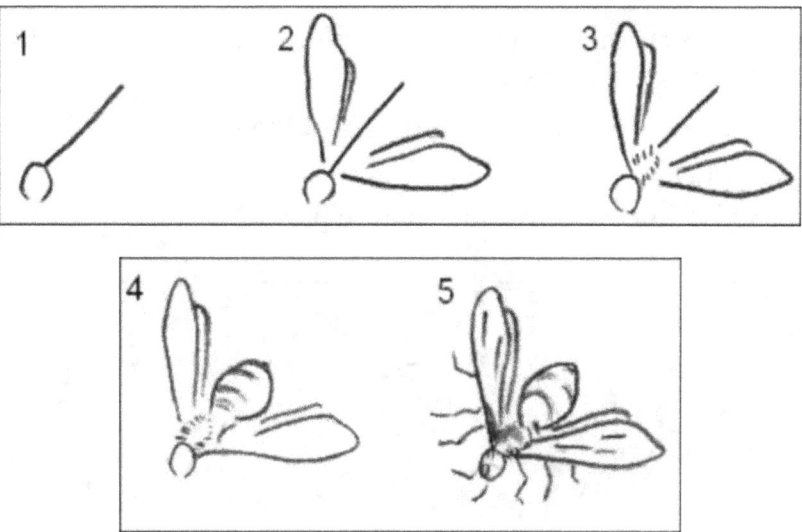

Ordinary things become special in an artist's world because an artist learns to see differently.

Your eyes become trained to observe, your hand to draw and your mind is constantly unfolding through perception, thought and expression.

The more you get into drawing, the more you learn to appreciate and love the beauty found in all things. With constant practice, drawing will become as natural as writing or talking.

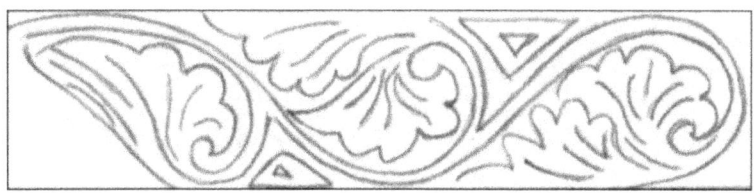

15 - IMAGINING LINES

METHOD SIX

Sketching a flower is made easier by imagining a line that goes through the flower (to get an idea of presentation).

Visualize and record the main direction of the stems with a single line.

The flower below is a Fuchsia where the 'middle' line helps to break down the subject into doable and separate parts.

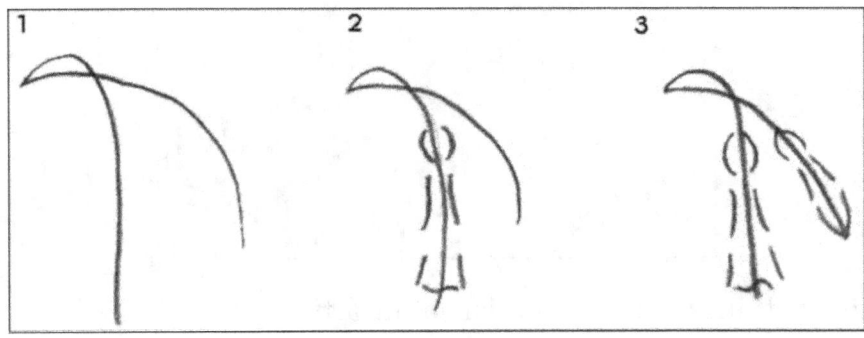

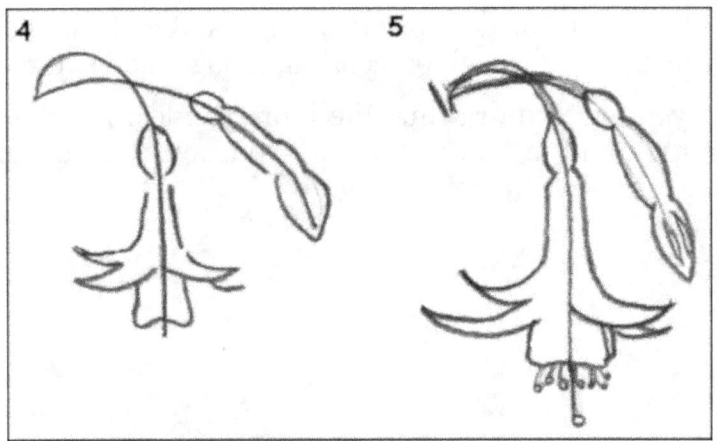

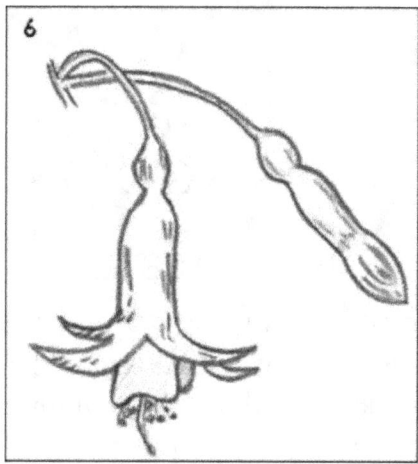

Practice creating drawings with the first and most basic line.

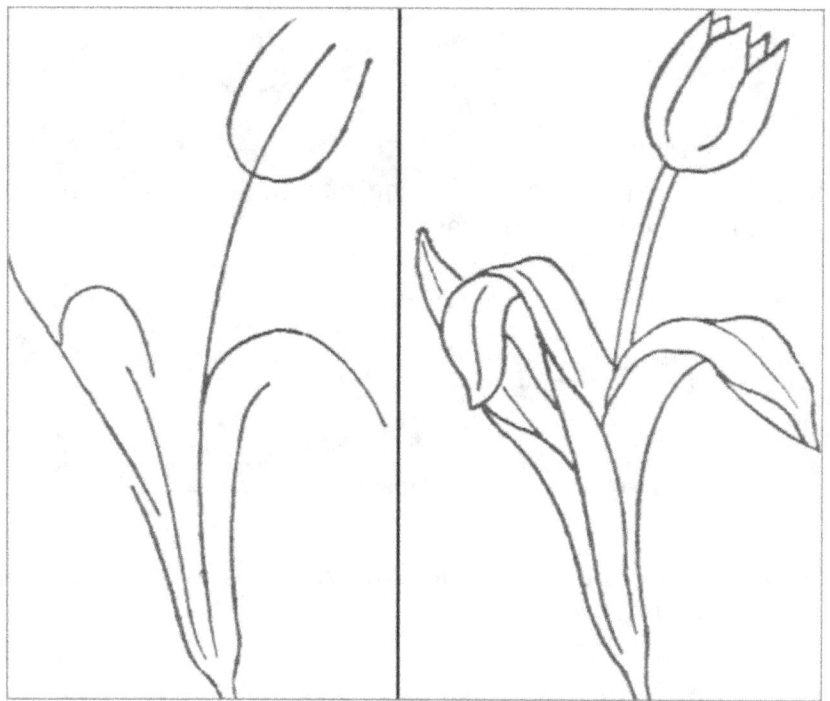

16 - USING DOTS

METHOD SEVEN

Another way to help you start a drawing is to use a series of dots.

Do you remember the dot to dot books we had as kids? This is an excellent way to help you get into the rhythm of nice flowing lines.

In the first example, this is what happens if you keep your eye on the pencil.

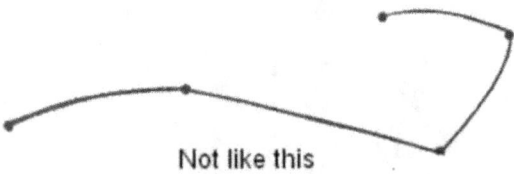

Not like this

The idea is to make an easy-flowing curved line, as in the following example, from the first dot to the last.

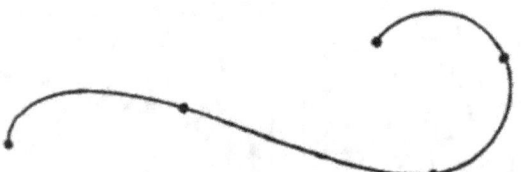

Like this, in one continuous flowing curve

Forget the pencil-point, instead look ahead to the next dot and envisage a curved line going through those dots.

Set up your own practice pages by making dots at different distances apart. Do this drawing exercise anywhere and anytime.

You can use dots as height and width measure points for any subject and create your own dot-to-dot picture. Make the marks very light so you can draw over them without erasing.

To draw a straight line, mark dots on your paper. If the distance is short, you will only need 2 dots but if it is quite long, a series of dots will help you obtain a near perfect straight line.

17 - FUN MEMORY DRAWING EXERCISE

METHOD EIGHT

There are numerous drawing exercises available to us and they are all generally good fun, including this one.

The challenge is to draw a pig with one single line and *with your eyes closed*!

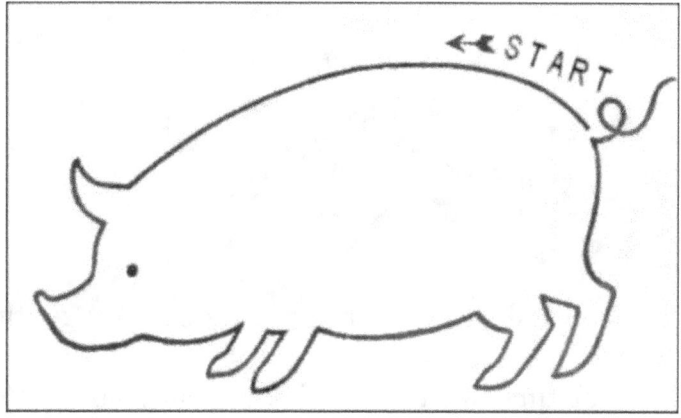

This exercise forces you to hold and keep the picture of the pig in your mind. It strengthens your ability to see things in your mind's eye and teaches you how to use your inner vision.

There's no harm in copying the pig a few times first, to become familiar with the form.

Here is my first attempt of the pig produced with a single line and with eyes closed...

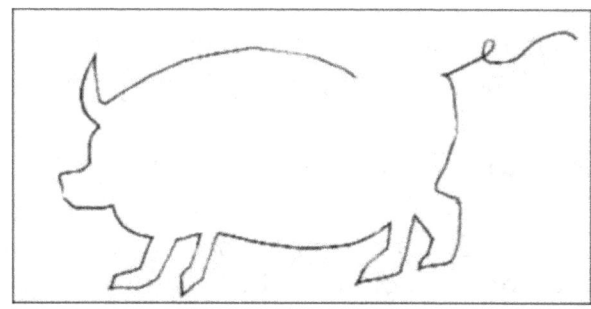

18 - PRACTICE BY COPYING

It's a great idea to continuously copy easy drawings created by other artists. I don't care what anyone says, I know for a fact that I taught myself to draw this way.

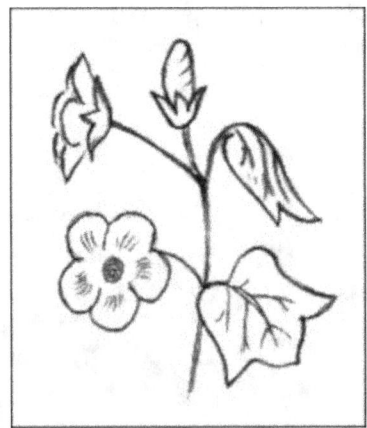

It really is a successful way of learning and once you get the hang of it, instead of copying exactly, just copy their ideas!

It is certainly not time wasted and it has many advantages, with the biggest being shown how to reduce complex forms into simple outlines.

I once read a book about the psychology of drawing and studies showed the usual order of learning to draw from child to adult is:

1 - Aimless scribble.

2 - Scribbling and imitating movements.

3 - Understanding pictures but not drawing beyond simple features and scribble.

4 - Copying from others to see how to get the right effects in the use of lines.

5 - Picture-writing, illustrated stories, scenes, etc.

6 - Studying technique of drawing, perspective, proportion, shading, etc.

So you see, regardless of our age, the learning order and progression remains the same.

I realized that once I gained confidence through copying, it was a natural step to venture outdoors and draw nature. I was armed with all that knowledge from other artists.

It doesn't matter if you are drawing from a book or drawing from nature, you follow the same process!

You learn to see everything in a simplified manner and nothing can stand in your way from drawing whatever you want.

The following images are supplied for you to copy and are designed to get you into the habit of practicing and copying all things that appeal to you. Your confidence grows with this practice.

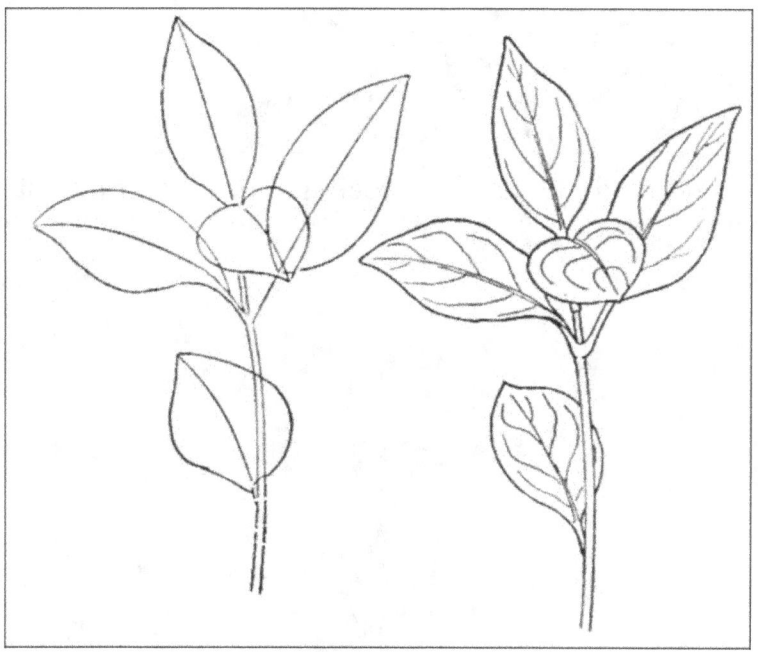

Common grass is a great drawing topic for all beginner artists. You come to see and realize the delicate perfection of growth, grace and beauty.

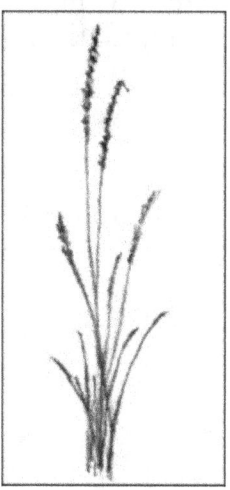

Some grasses stand stiff and straight, some droop and some sway gracefully in a breeze. Pick a small section of grass and magnify it to make intriguing artwork, just like you see below, where an 8B pencil was used to achieve the blackest black.

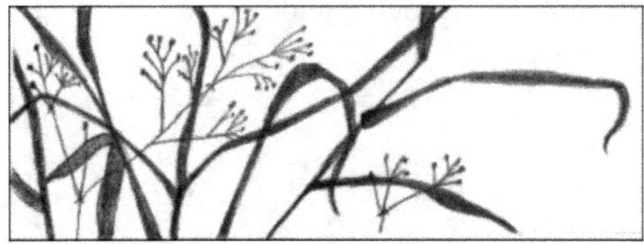

Use your preferred method (i.e. block-in, dots, etc.) to construct any of these drawings.

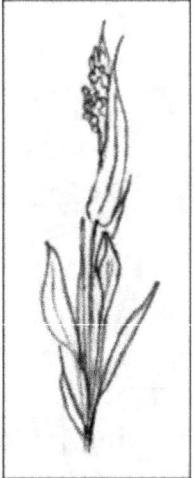

There are so many benefits to drawing, it definitely stimulates mental activity, accurate observation and initiative.

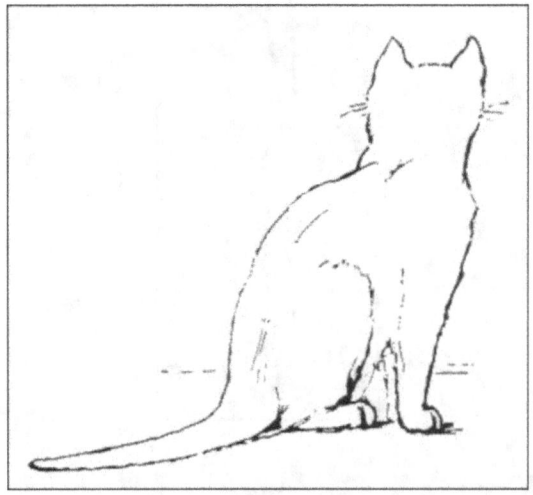

If you have the patience to teach yourself and persist, you will be delightfully rewarded in a variety of ways.

Outline drawing can express every single quality of an object except its color - that's pretty clever, isn't it?

In the next drawing, see the small parallel lines used to portray the shadow of leaves upon leaves. It's simple but effective and just right for trainee artists. This is called "half tone" or "half tint". If you place the lines closer together, the area appears darker.

However, when you first start to draw, don't be concerned with anything other than obtaining a good resemblance. There is plenty of time to expand your knowledge and doing it slowly builds a more solid foundation. Besides, it is more enjoyable if you learn in your own good time and to advance when your interest is stimulated in new areas.

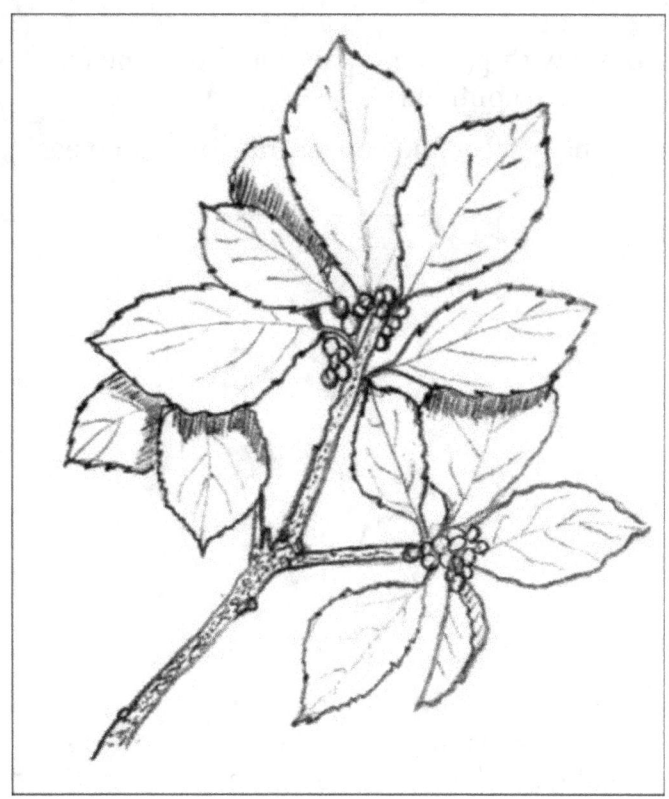

* To block in this drawing, set down the main stem line first.

* Next, observe and record the angles where the branches leave the main stem and the angles of the leaves on their stalks.

* The general direction of the leaf outlines are blocked in with light, straight lines.

* Once this is done, you can see the character in the leading lines and it is now a matter of drawing over your light lines to add more details and curves to the image.

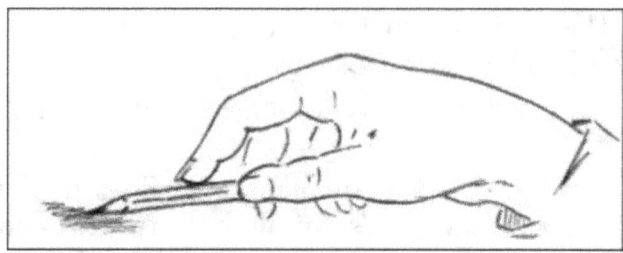

Always carry paper and pencil with you so you can draw whenever the mood strikes. Draw anything like single objects or parts of objects because all types of practice counts towards your progress.

When you draw small pieces of things that attract you, that helps identify the real you and what your innermost wishes and desires really are.

Just mess around with pencil on paper and become comfortable, which in turn makes you more confident.

Forget about being perfect and concentrate only on pleasing yourself.

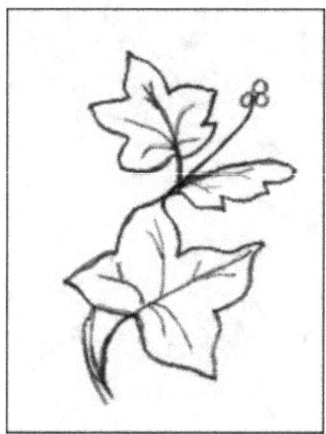

Produce little outline sketches in 30 seconds or less and then progress onto small shaded images in a minute or less. These are wonderful sessions that indicate how far you have advanced. Vary this test with some simple topics and then try some that are a little more difficult.

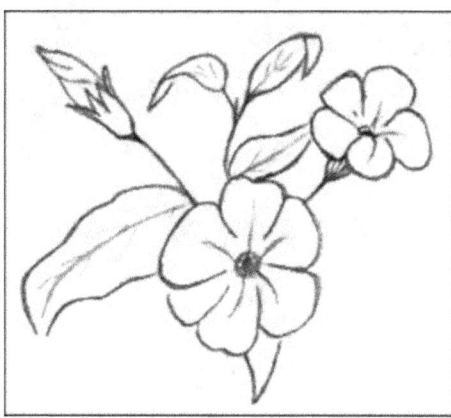

Despite what anyone says, it is ok to copy other artists while you are learning because this helps you find a style that you particularly like and enjoy creating. You don't have to follow in their footsteps but you can keep to the same road!

It is important to be influenced by as many artists as possible so you can pull the most interesting aspects from that variety of work. Bit by bit, these influences contribute to a more personal style that is uniquely you.

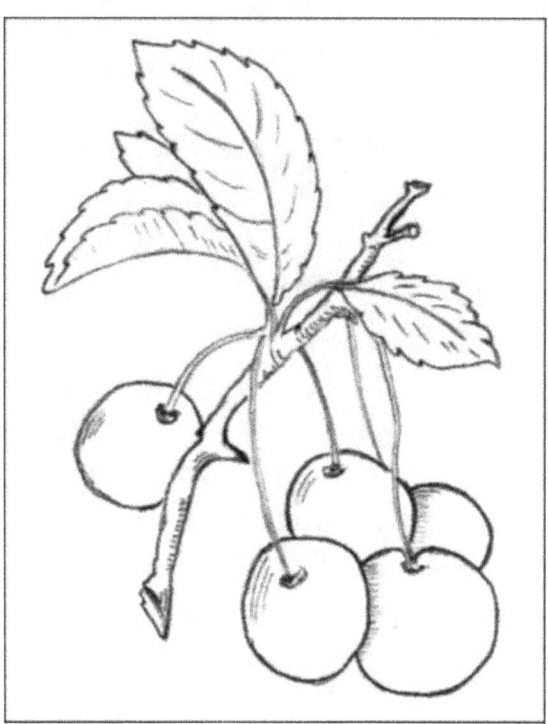

Keep copying and practicing!

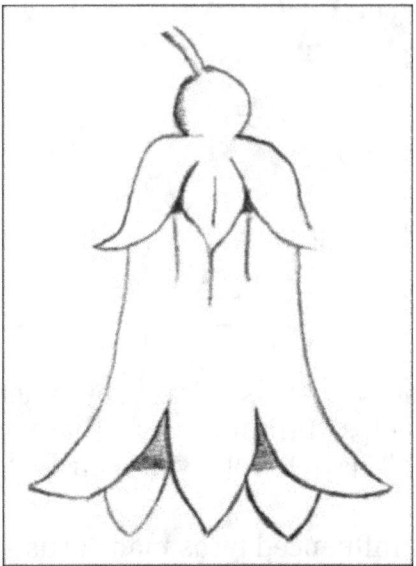

At first, you won't be entirely satisfied with your results but you can expect and therefore accept that without becoming disheartened.

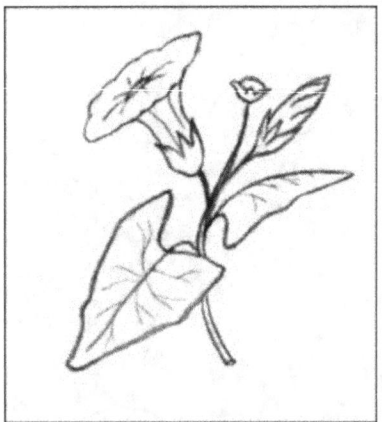

It doesn't take long before you master these most basic skills and art becomes a natural part of your new life.

19 - DRAWING AND SKETCHING NATURE – BOOK 3

INTRODUCTION

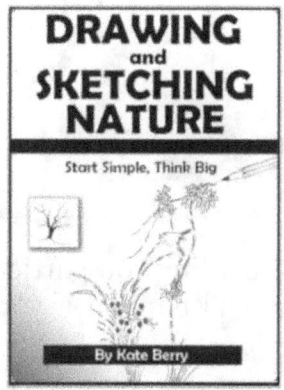

Are you ready to get serious about sketching from nature?

The purpose of this book is to provide self-instruction that will lead you to gradually rely entirely upon your own skill. From here, you can advance as far as you want to and really it can't get more exciting than that!

The best way to learn anything is to start simple. This allows your understanding as well as your skills to grow in tune with each other. Just add repetitive action and it then becomes a habit. When you're finished here, you will know how to quickly and successfully sketch plant-life in its basic form - and with confidence!

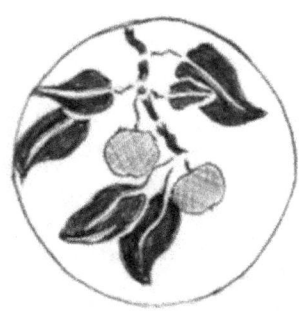

It's hard to say which is the best pencil for you but I use a 2B because it can be light or dark, depending on the pressure applied. I also like the fine lines of a mechanical pencil so it's used in most examples, along with photocopy paper because of its smooth surface.

The majority of instruction refers to linear drawing and sketching to keep the contents easy to follow and digest. My hope is to lead you to a successful result by the simplest means. There are only a few things that you need to remember but they apply to every object occurring in Nature.

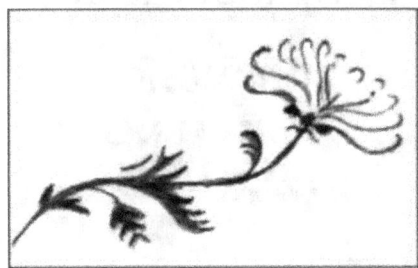

Your skills will advance providing you participate in these exercises and it's no surprise that nothing will happen if you don't. Good results don't come through luck.

By taking action, your confidence takes you from small beginnings to an 'anything is possible' attitude.

This section continues to build upon what you have learned so far and it is assumed that you are comfortable forming general outlines with a sure hand.

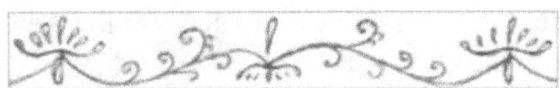

20 - OVERCOMING INSECURITY

I can completely relate to any insecurity you may feel, so I urge you to take heart in the fact that every step you take is a step in the right direction.

Your path will be different to mine because you have different tastes, wants and needs so here are a few little tips to help you move forward:

1. Dedicate some time to practice drawing a confident firm line. Try to make lines with one sweep of your hand. Feeble, unsure lines keep you in a state of uncertainty so the sooner you leave them behind, the faster your confidence grows.

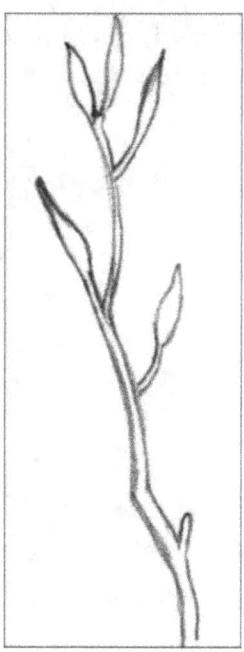

2. Embrace mistakes because they are the teachers that help you progress and learn faster.

3. Study little parts before trying to portray a whole subject. For beginner artists, a whole landscape is daunting so be mindful to first select one thing to draw, then move on to 2 things and so on.

Focus on gradually building up your confidence just by sketching little bits and you'll soon see that it's not so hard. You become encouraged which furthers your sense of adventure - it's like a rolling stone so please do allow things to roll and see what happens.

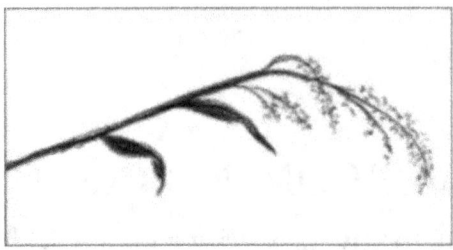

A carefree attitude is important. There is so much information on learning how to draw or sketch but it's quite possible to illustrate anything once you give yourself permission to just have a go, regardless of how much knowledge you have.

If you learn gradually like so many of us have done in the past, your sketching skills will improve and advance, all of their own accord.

Look, I still think there is a lot I need to learn but the fact is I am confident enough to portray anything even though I was never a very confident person. It is by doing that I am here at this place passing on information that I found helpful, to you.

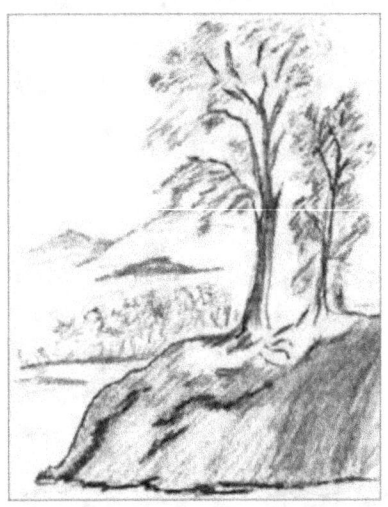

Hopefully, this material will provide a stepping stone that piques your interest even more and inspires you to keep investigating what there is to know. Slowly but surely always wins the race.

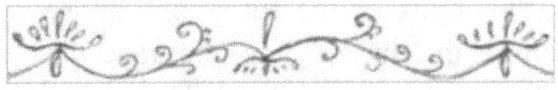

21 - WHAT TO SKETCH

Make a point to sketch things that you find appealing. If you have a great love of the outdoors and you only want to sketch landscapes, then by all means concentrate all your efforts in that area. Take artistic advice only if you agree with it, otherwise ignore it. You are in control of how and what you want to draw.

> TIP: There is no point forcing yourself to sketch unattractive things because you'll put your pencil down in sheer disinterest and never likely pick it up again.

This is important if drawing is something that you really want to do!

When I first started, I forced myself to do still life exercises because it was recommended in several drawing books. Back then, I wasn't stimulated by still life and I lost the incentive to draw. A long time elapsed before I finally retrieved my pencils but from then on I only focused on interesting subjects and therefore kept up a good momentum of improving skills. I hope you can learn from my lost time and remember to always follow your instinct.

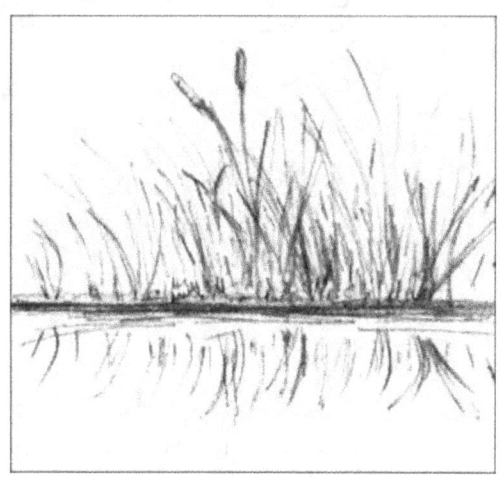

You know your preferences so stick with them while you learn the basics of drawing and sketching. There is plenty of time for experimentation into other areas later.

22 - SINGLE ITEMS

Each illustration is a dedicated sketch or drawing which simply means it is done with a close-up point of view.

Study of the different drawings shows how to translate nature into outline.

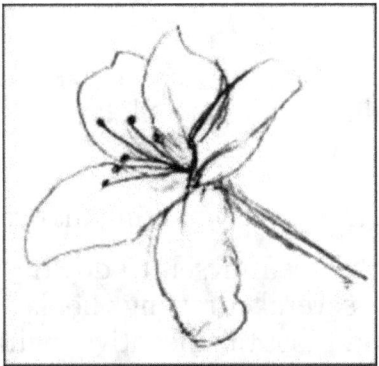

Draw lightly when commencing a sketch because the first lines are trial lines. Many of the illustrations here still have light guidelines but the good lines have been darkened for better viewing.

To begin the first exercise, select a common no-frills leaf from outdoors.

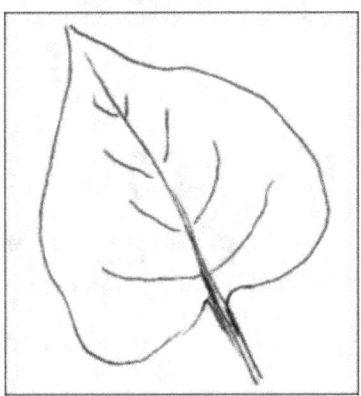

Place it on sketch paper and make tiny marks to indicate the height and width. These markers give you a boundary to work within and all you have to do is follow the contour of the leaf and meet up with each mark along the way.

Sometimes this little exercise is an eye-opener because the real size is different to what you perceive. All of these exercises help to erase perceptions and you learn to "see" the way an artist does.

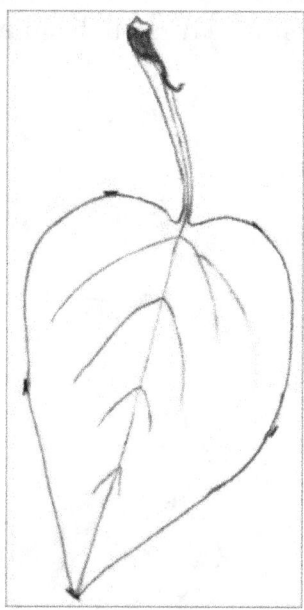

The above example is a Devils Ivy leaf from my garden. Using the leaf, I made 5 marks (left obvious in the image) - 2 at the top, 2 for the sides and 1 at the bottom.

Of course, you can copy these examples but the experience of drawing from a real leaf is of more benefit to you in the long run.

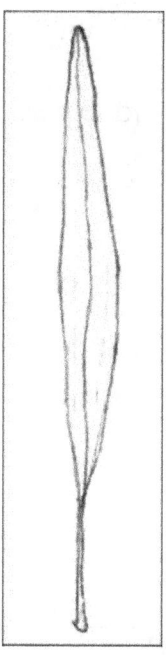

Repeat the experiment using leaves of all shapes and sizes.

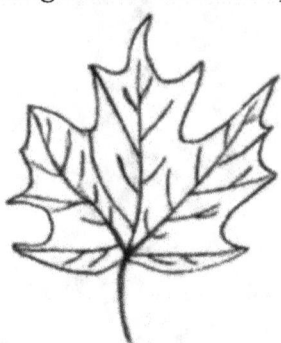

Ok, you've drawn a leaf more than once and you're good to move on, right?

Now let's try sketching out a single clover...

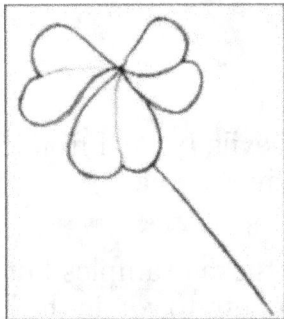

I aim to draw a cluster later on so this is merely preparation work to become familiar with shapes. For now, we stay concentrating on single items only.

Keep the momentum going and experiment with different aspects of a clover...

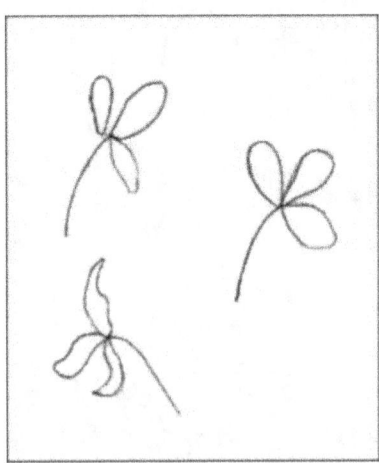

For the sake of progress and interest, it's time to try a flower. This time I used a kind of block-in method around each petal to help form the overall shape.

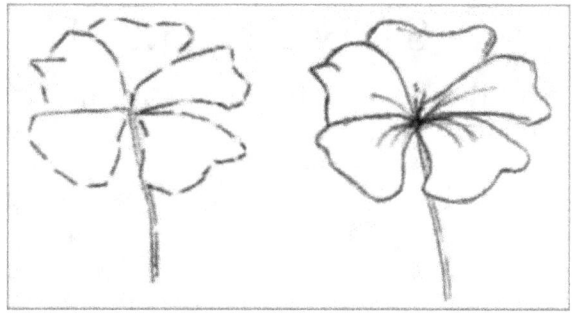

All flowers are different so turn them around to find the simplest view.

The side view of an Azalea (below) is the easiest aspect for us newbies.

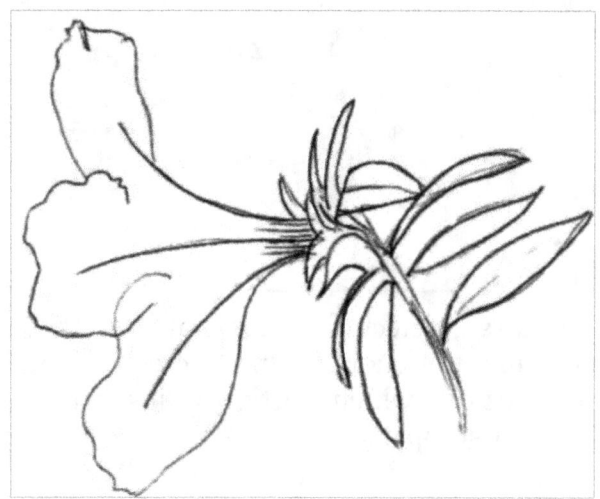

Reminder:

You actually need to DO these exercises to be able to sketch Nature. I repeat this because it's just not possible to know how to draw after simply reading 'how to' books.

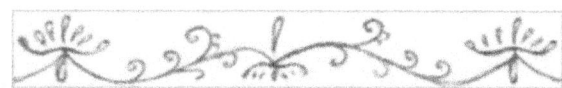

23 - STEM AND LEAF

The next exercise is the combination of stem and leaf with a closer examination of the joint.

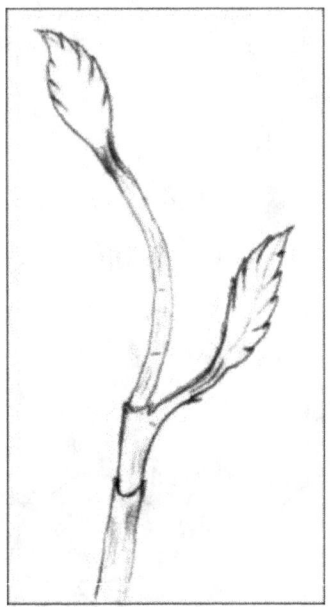

If a plant is too large, select the most interesting part of the plant. Occasionally, there's just not enough time to create a whole image, so just take a moment to consider which portion grabs your interest and do a dedicated sketch of that snippet.

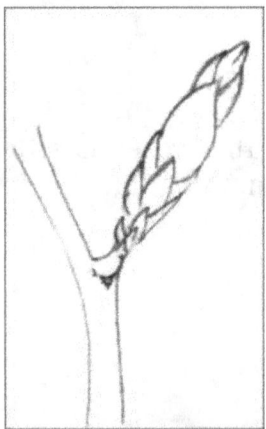

Concentrate on observing - you don't have to know the names of all types of leaves but good observation reveals that some are round, oval or heart-shaped and some have smooth or broken edges. Even if you don't know what sort of plant it is, it will be recognized and admired all the same because your portrayal is true.

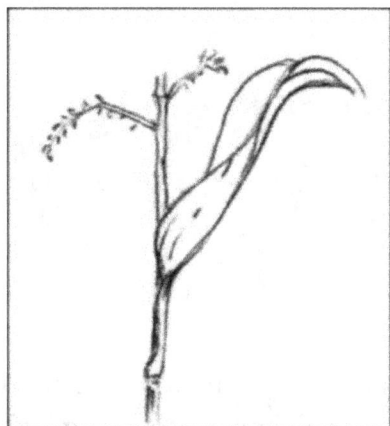

Notice how leaves grow and how each one has a kind of grace all its own. Ask yourself - how are the leaves attached to the stem? Do any leaves point upwards? Do any point straight out towards the margin? Notice the stem and any change in size.

With a few suggestive lines, transfer the image to paper. Drawing is simply a seeing of relations. Use your sketchbook to record the way you think and see.

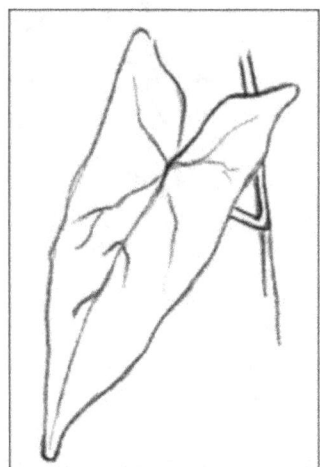

The next images are a progression from a single leaf to several plain leaves on a single stem.

There was no way I was going to try to portray a fern exactly so this next image is the perception of how it appeared. My main aim was to get the general flow and shape of most leaves.

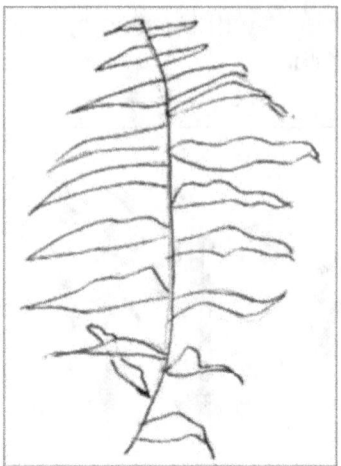

The first thing you do is draw a line to represent the angle of the stem.

TIP: If you want some thickness to a stem, place some broken lines parallel to the first lightly sketched line - this is a great way to manage the proper thickness. Trying to draw a continuous even line parallel to another isn't so easy (and can be discouraging) so it's good to remember this tip whenever you need to draw parallel lines.

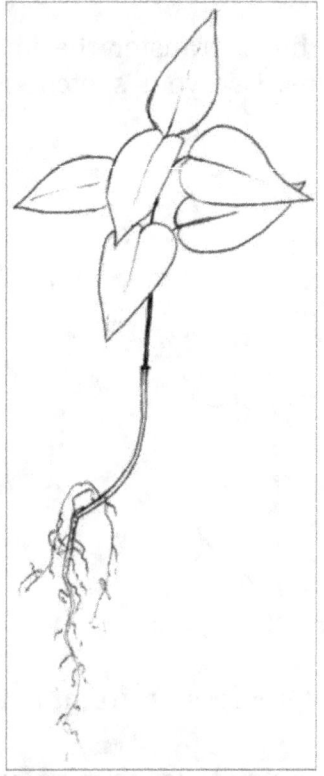

Estimate the distance (from the bottom) where the leaves begin on the stem and roughly sketch in the shape of them. If starting from the top works better for you, go ahead and do that.

If you misjudge the layout, keep drawing in light lines to get the feel of the formation of leaves. Any changes you make to a sketch are done by inserting new lines, try to get out of the habit of erasing and instead develop the habit to re-draw incorrect lines (it's good training).

There's no need to copy anything exactly, use perception for things like intricate roots and scribble them in to portray an overall effect.

If you do the same subject more than once, it's amazing what you learn and how the next illustration is much better than the previous one.

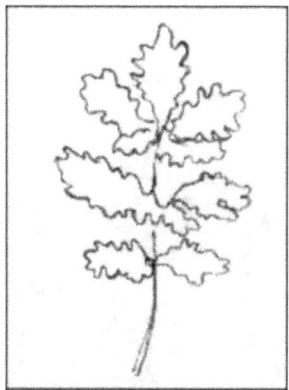

Drawing something two or three times in different positions is better than doing one that is more complicated. Once you master a simple subject like this, your confidence grows and you're ready to move on to attack the next challenge.

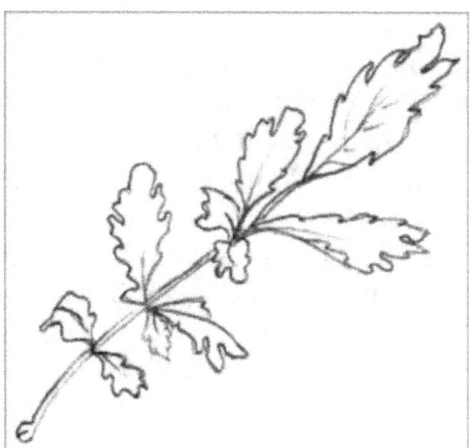

If you pick a specimen from the garden and take it indoors to sketch, place a similar sized piece of sketch paper beneath the plant and again use that as a guide to make the appropriate marks on your sketch paper where the plant sits within the 'frame'.

You can judge with reasonable accuracy the position of the stem and indicate a similar position on your paper. Mark the highest point and the extreme right and left. If there are some buds or berries, roughly position some extra marks next to the ones already in place.

The placement of plant on paper helps you determine whether the stem starts vertically or how much it slants to the right or left.

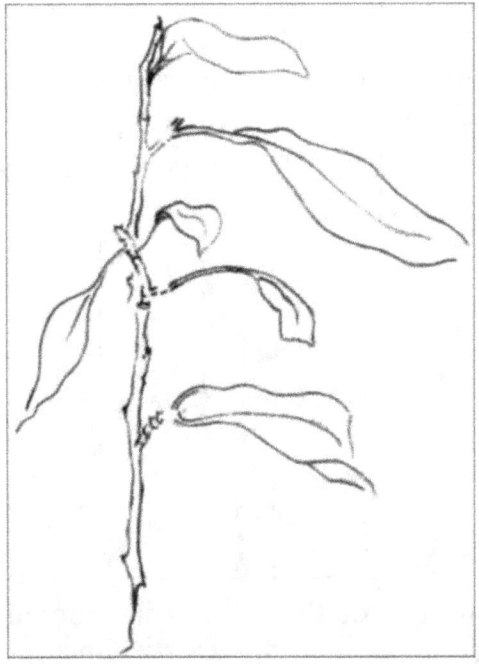

Using a quick, light sketch line, indicate first the stem and then the first leaf or branch from the bottom, guessing at the length or point on the stem where it begins.

A little study of the joint comes next, noting the way the leaf or branch merges with the main stem. You only need to do this for close-up drawings but this inside knowledge helps you in many ways in the future.

Draw the stem as dark as it looks between blossoms and leaves, and check for any change in size. Find where a shoot commences its journey and which way it goes to find the sunshine. Search for highlights like this and if appealing, make them the point of emphasis.

TIP: Judge the angle of each leaf against the main stem or use the vertical and horizontal sides of the paper to gauge positions.

As you practice and progress, you become familiar or comfortable with using the sides of paper, original main lines or a border to assist you with placement. These are your 'silent' helpers.

This type of practice enables you to create thoughtful and independent work. The ultimate aim of all artists is to express their individual vision and not to be just another imitator.

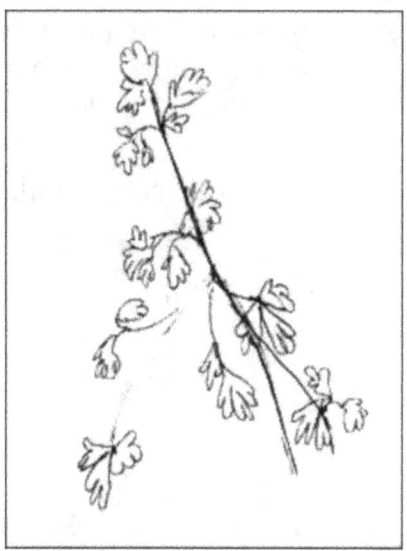

The above sketch was done on a whim, with pen on scrap paper. I don't know how to describe the feeling of staring at your own creation, especially if you're like me and you've spent the majority of your life thinking you can't draw. It doesn't matter that it's not a masterpiece but I know this particular image exists nowhere else in the world!

The next exercise is to sketch another simple plant but this time look closer and take note of a combination of things:

1. line of growth

2. pose or gesture

3. contours

4. texture

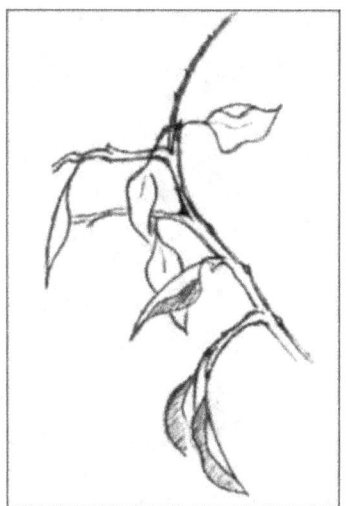

With practice, you come to get a feeling for the flow of lines so this kind of study is very valuable.

Observation becomes a natural reaction once you know what to look for and do it a few times over. Copying strengthens your observation skills. By gradually building up your knowledge, you also build your internal make-up as an artist.

Let's discuss the preceding points in more detail...

1. The line of growth:

Observe whether the main lines of a plant are straight or curved, and whether they are vertical, horizontal or oblique in position. (The most accomplished artist never disregards lines of action.)

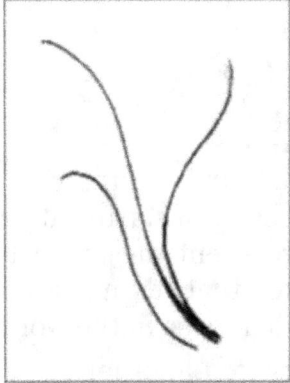

2. The pose or gesture:

Study the size and shapes of parts. Once you know the general direction of a stalk or stem, next take notice of the length and width of the leaf and the relative size of the flower. (Artists always need to study proportions.)

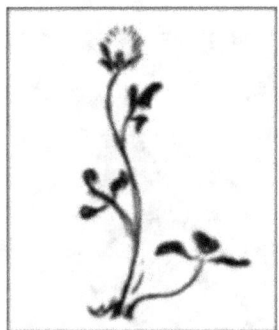

3. The contours:

Notice how appearances change when you observe them from different angles. To see and successfully record the effects of foreshortening demands a keener eye than any other exercise. It takes a bit of effort but you'll succeed simply by practicing. A simple plant is the perfect thing to teach you the fundamental problems of appearance drawing (foreshortening).

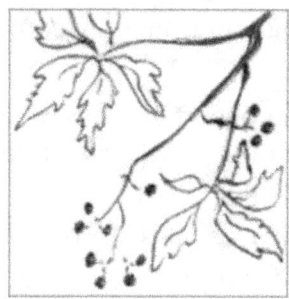

4. Structure:

Study the structure and how each part relates to others. This exercise requires even closer observation because the details are smaller and less distinct. In plant drawing, the test of an artist's power is the joint, just as it is in drawing the human figure.

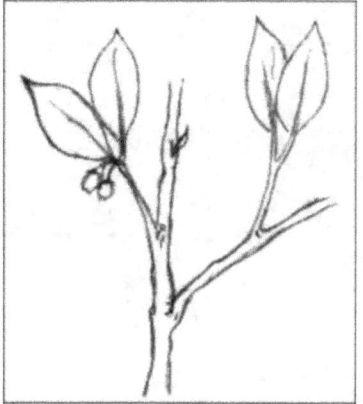

Don't be shy about giving significance to every line and dot in a dedicated sketch.

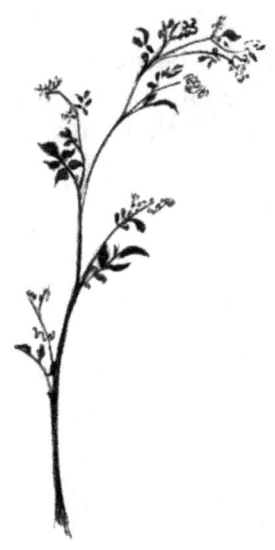

TIP: Work your way through an image by comparing the size of one line with the next.

Judging the length of line becomes a habit as you continue to compare one line to another. By doing this, you take care of proportion and perspective and it's all through your own observation skills!

Once you finish a practice session with one plant, it's time to turn it around and repeat the same exercise from a different point of view. If you feel reluctant to do this, remember the original rule to follow your instinct and stay with things that interest you. There's no obligation but depending on how serious you are, you'll probably return to complete this exercise sometime in the future.

Remember the single clover leaf? Now try copying the outline of a cluster...

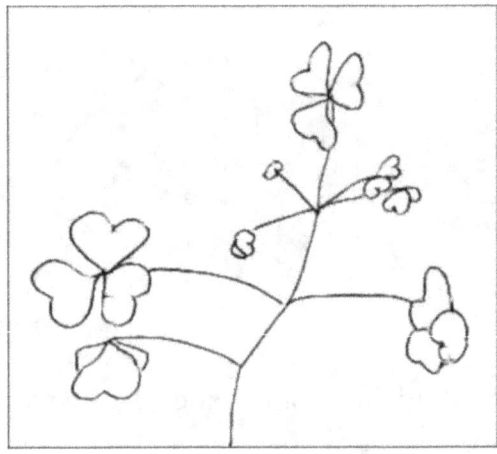

It's a little more complicated because all leaves don't face forward and they go in all different directions. Perspective is taken care of when you draw the shapes you see. Sketch how each leaf really appears and ignore the little voice inside your head that says it doesn't look right! Once you see the finished illustration, everything looks as it should.

I should mention here that this particular image is not a display of good composition (that's discussed later) but it doesn't matter when practicing, just draw anything in all different ways.

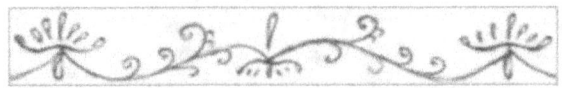

24 - STEM, LEAF AND FLOWER

To begin, lightly sketch in (or block-in) the overall outside shape of the flower and leaves and take note of the vertical or angular stem.

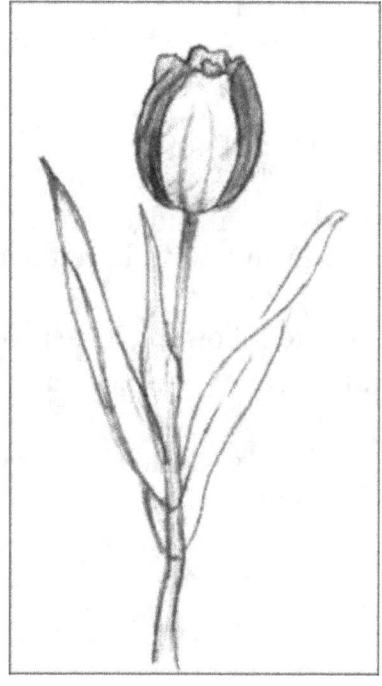

Don't worry about being neat, roughly put in some light lines to get an image down as best you can. It doesn't take long to erase unwanted lines if you want a good drawing.

Check if the stem is the right size overall and if the leaves are comparable in size to the flower, bulb or berries.

Above, the bulb is one inch deep and the total height of the drawing is roughly 4 inches so you just estimate that the bulb fits into the height 4 times to get similar proportions.

Next is another example of a blocked-in sprig which helps to place parts where they belong.

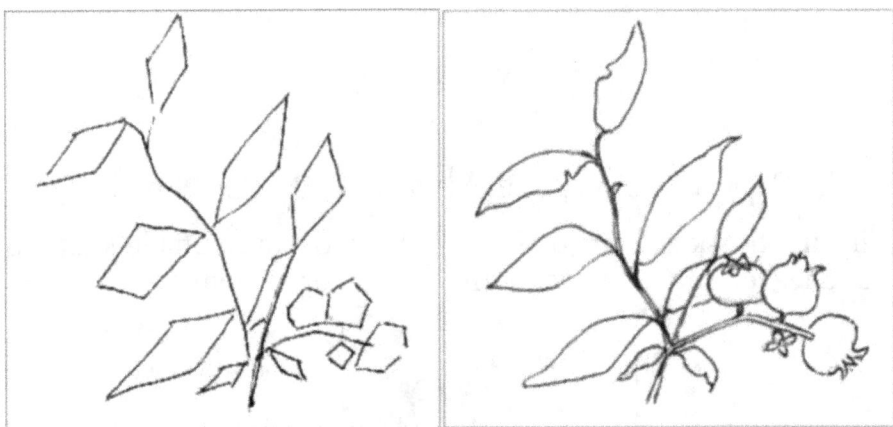

It's only a matter of going over those light block-in lines and adding curves to form each item properly.

Work with confidence and then judge if you portrayed these points correctly in your illustration. You always have the option to sketch in new lines.

Here's a simple procedure to follow to create a sketch:

1. Indicate the general direction of the main stem/s with very light strokes.

2. Touch the paper only here and there to suggest the general shapes and positions of the different parts.

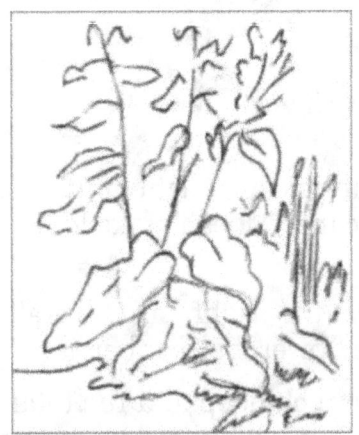

3. Indicate the thickness of each important stem.

4. Now go over it all again and emphasize a leaf-edge here or a bit of shadow there.

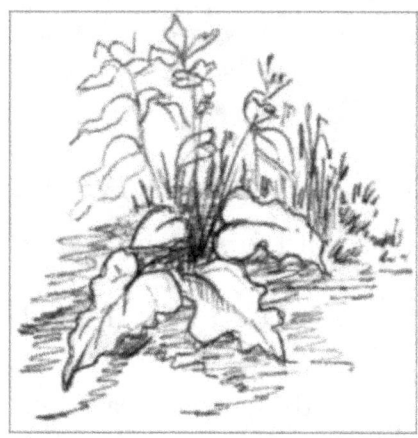

5. Depict texture by using a delicate continuous line in some places and a heavy broken one in others.

When you draw lightly and quickly, speed removes awkwardness and uncertainty. This is where surprises happen because it allows a certain kind of free-flow when your mind is taken out of the equation. There is no time for thought when you have to draw quickly - go and try that out now to see what I mean - it's a revelation!

The image below was created in one of my "quick" practice sessions some time ago. It worked itself out because I concentrated only on outlining the true shapes of each item.

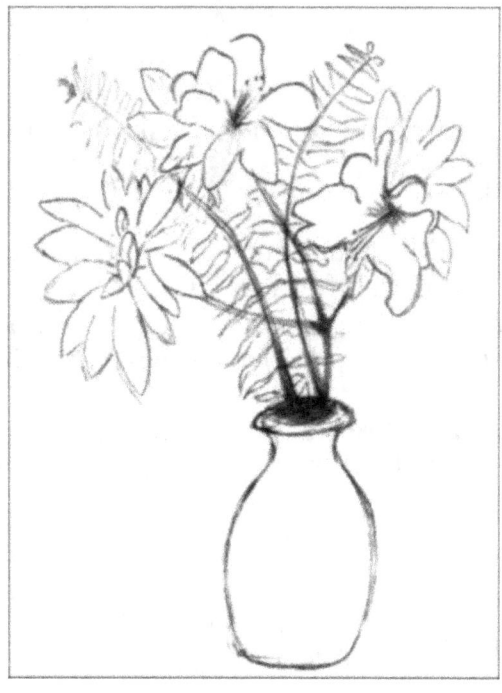

25 - PERSPECTIVE OF LEAF AND FLOWER

Perspective is just another word for the appearance of things. It can be a complex topic to learn in theory but if you learn as you go, it won't be any trouble to master portraying it. Don't let it intimidate you, all you have to do is trust your eyes.

A sketch is simply the recording of an idea. Ideas of form or appearance in our minds are usually very vague and therefore we don't think about foreshortened appearances or items in perspective until we give them special attention.

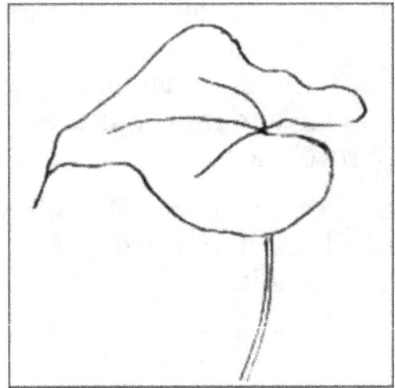

In nature, leaves are foreshortened in the majority of cases.

Here's your exercise:

Find a simple curling leaf (no fancy edges) and draw the actual shape around the outside. Don't be afraid to draw it exactly as it appears. Now place the leaf beside your sketch. Squint your eyes to better see the darker shape of the leaf against the paper so you see the real shape.

How did you go? If your sketch is nothing like it, just do it again, concentrating on the actual outline of the leaf against the paper.

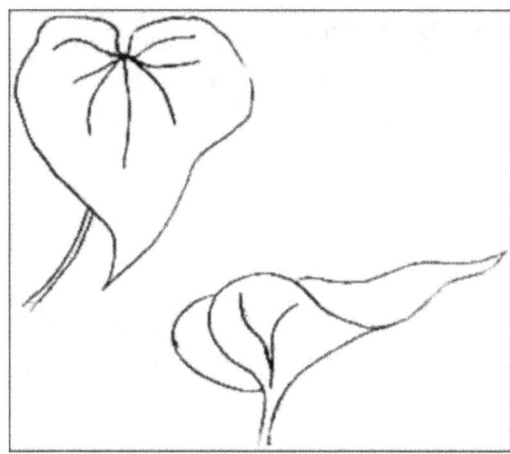

Foreshortening is a term used to describe a distorted perspective.

Practice sketching leaves edgewise to get the hang of foreshortened aspects. Also try it with the stem pointing toward you and away from you.

Repeatedly practice each new position to learn to see correctly. This is great training and you really benefit by devoting some time to this exercise.

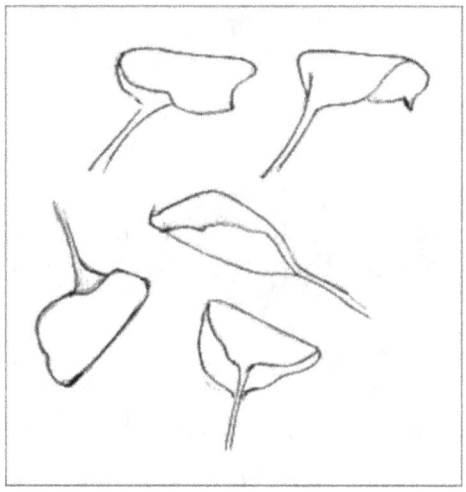

Another great trick to understand perspective and the effects of foreshortening is to draw a leaf on a piece of cardboard (roughly 3 inches long). Tilt the cardboard horizontally so that it becomes foreshortened and take particular notice of the limited detail that you actually see.

Here's my cardboard experiment:

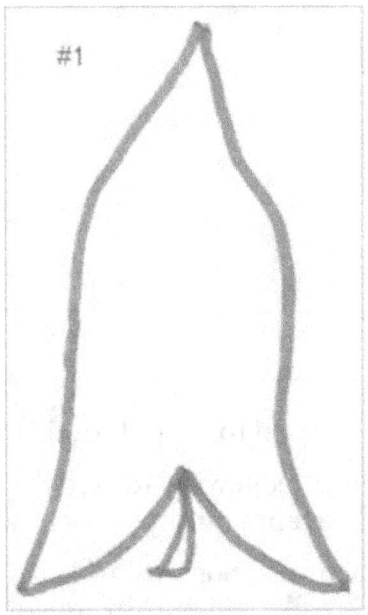

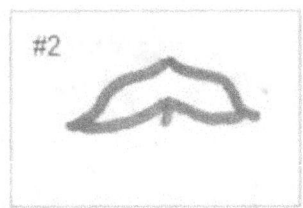

#1 is the front-on view of a full leaf drawing done in felt pen (to make the outline more obvious for this experiment). #2 is the view I saw after tilting the cardboard.

If you have a ruler, measure the foreshortened aspect. You know the cardboard is about 3 inches long and suddenly it only measures about a half or one inch, depending on how far you tilt it.

So now you know you only need to portray a fraction of the whole when observing from such an angle.

You don't have to do this exercise but it sure helps speed up the process of understanding the tricky topics of perspective and foreshortening.

Studying silhouettes is yet another way to see how a leaf looks when it's "coming toward you" or going back from the stem or curled over.

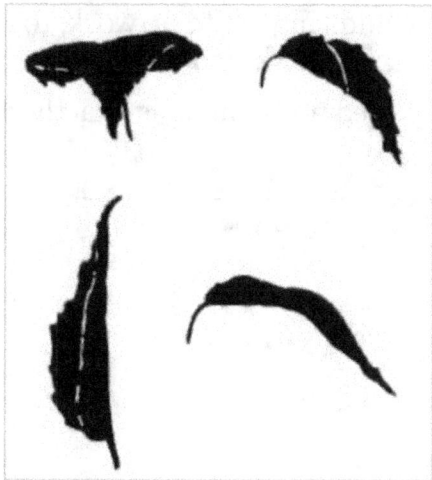

A silhouette is merely an outline filled with a solid color. They show only the general shape and outline without all the distracting details.

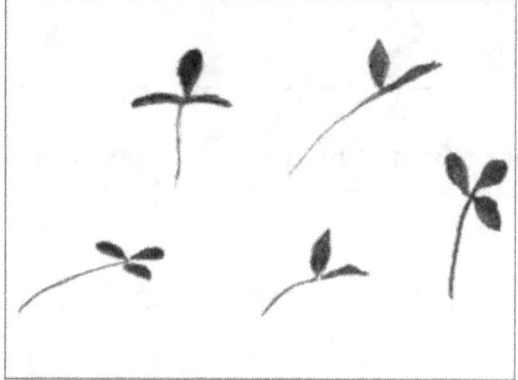

You can also see silhouettes by placing objects on a windowsill in the daytime and move far enough away so that no detail is visible.

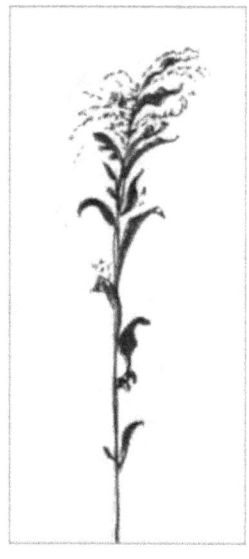

Drawing in silhouette adds impact to artwork, too. A 4B pencil makes it easier because it gives a thick, dark stroke.

Portraying flowers viewed at an angle is exactly the same procedure as for leaves.

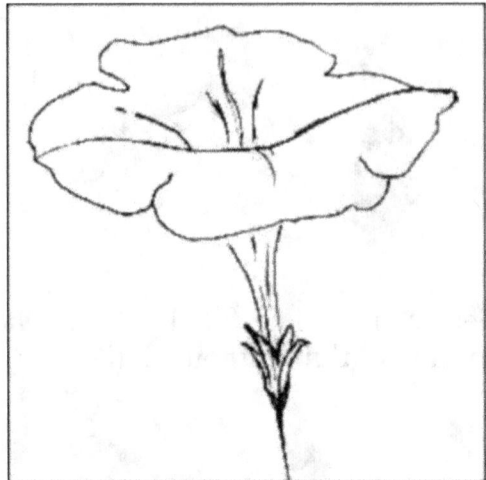

It's only a matter of estimating the size of the front portion that you see (closest to you), compared to the back.

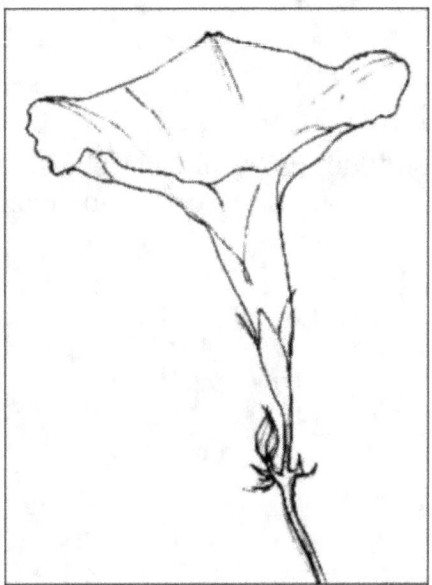

26 - TREES

Simply sketch a branch or two to become familiar with this form.

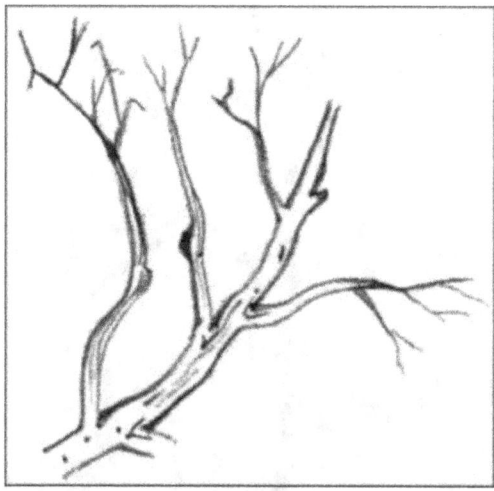

There's plenty to keep you occupied when you study branches - some are straight, some bend with their own weight and others are gnarled or not so regular.

An artist stands back to scrutinize the character and general profile of trees and even from a distance, can see the overall form and each tree's uniqueness.

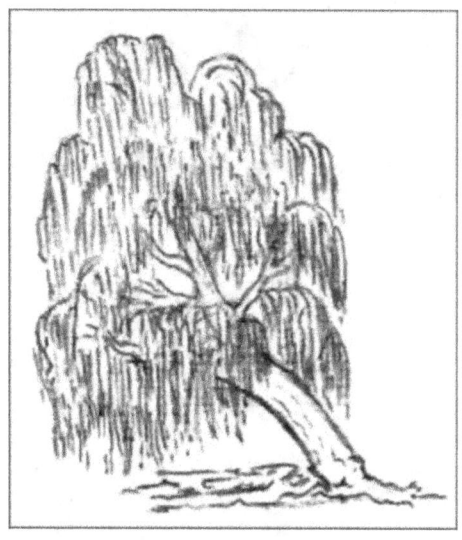

Once observed from a distance, note the strongest characteristics and try to move closer to find what else is different.

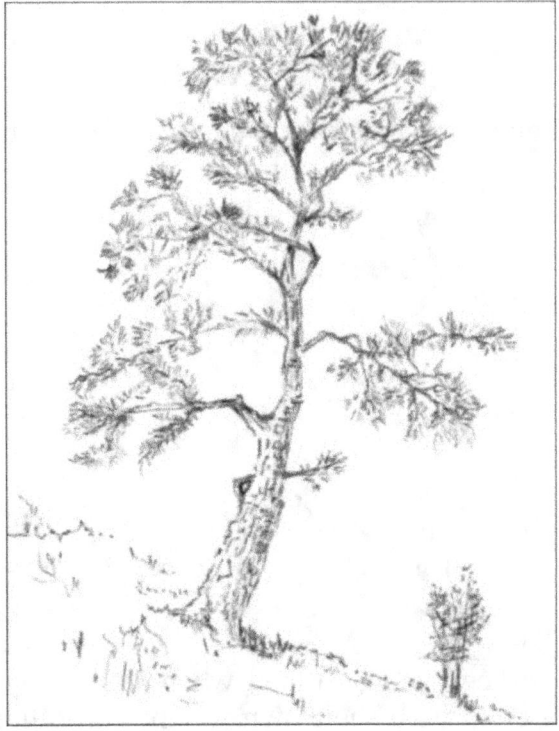

Notice the growth and progress of the trunk as well as checking if the leaves sit in clusters or are scattered.

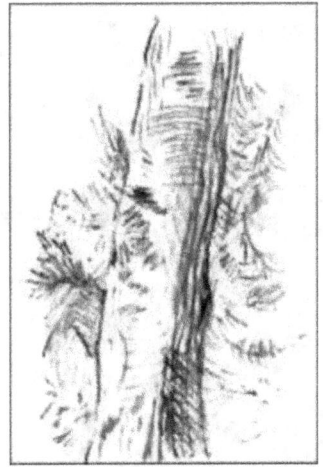

Obviously trees cannot be drawn exactly as they appear because there are millions of leaves and we can't possibly draw them all.

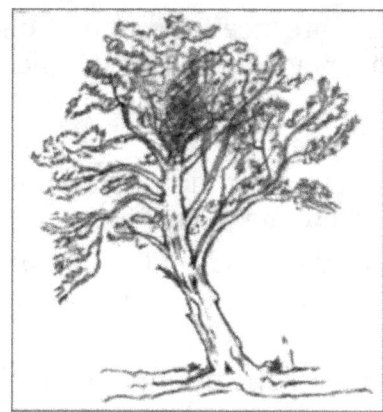

The best we can do is portray or suggest the differences from other kinds of trees and leave our audience to fill in details from their own knowledge.

So the main things are:

1. proportions,

2. general shape, and

3. the character of trunks.

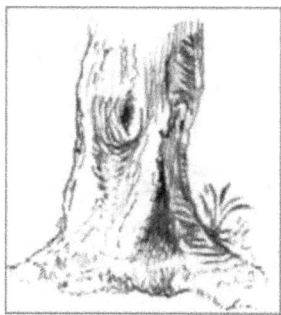

The most interesting forms for artists are the gnarled trunks, naked roots, and the way a tree twists in its efforts to grow.

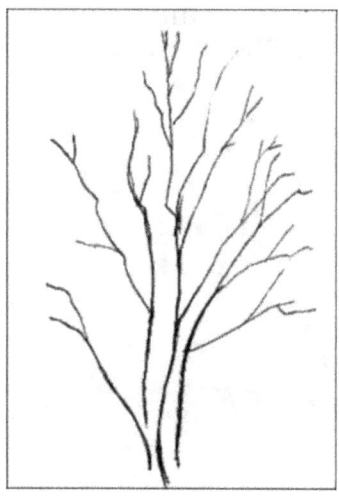

In this next image, there are trees at different distances. The first group is very near so they almost reach the top of the picture – this group sits on the first base line (horizontal and parallel with the bottom border or horizon).

There are some bushes close behind so a second base line was inserted further up from the line where the main trees sit.

The third group is smaller and indistinct because they are in the extreme distance so a third base line is inserted higher up from the other two.

The use of base lines is like a prompt to remind you to draw items smaller than those on the initial base line which is the point closest to you. All estimations are made against the main group in front.

Now draw a few light lines around the main shapes.

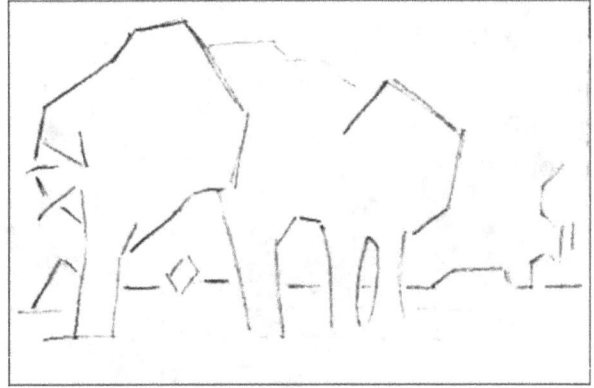

I don't keep with regular shapes like circles and squares for blocking in, I use lines at all angles to indicate the overall shape but that's entirely your preference.

If you do sketch after sketch like this, your calculations of relations becomes automatic.

You can squint your eyes to see differences in tone and make notes on the sketch which areas to keep light or dark.

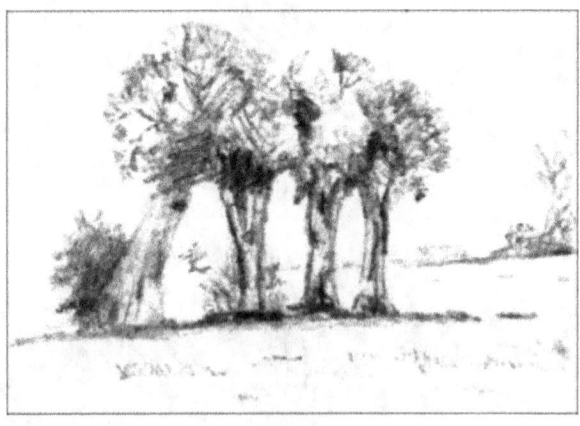

Using several base lines is a great way to assist you with the layout of a landscape drawing. Make sure you experiment with it to discover the myriad of ways it can benefit you.

For something different and because I still love experimenting, I used the side of the pencil as the first flat tone and went over it in a different direction to represent shadowed areas. You can do the same with the ground and reflections.

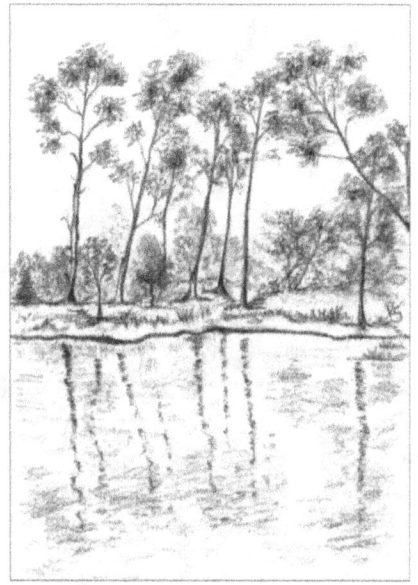

The sketch above was done completely with the side of the lead, it's very rough but I remember being surprised when it turned out as well as it did. That is why I encourage you to try different things, it's amazing what you discover about your true capabilities.

The next chapter explains composition which means we need to think about the size and position of the paper for a particular tree you want to sketch. For example, a pine tree is a typical vertical sketch.

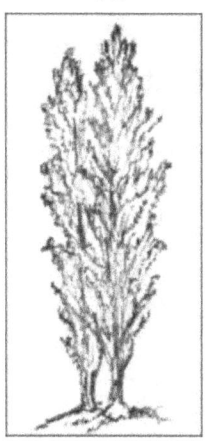

The effect of foliage is achieved by squiggly lines going in the direction of branches which gives the perception of a certain appearance. In art, nothing is ever quite how it really appears.

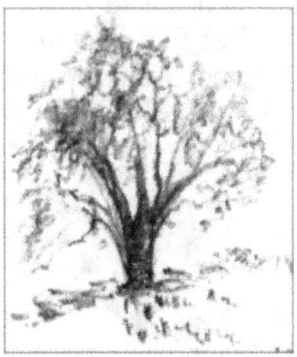

Winter is the perfect time for studying the main lines of growth and no distraction with leaves.

I drew a lot of trees in silhouette when I was learning because I knew I could do a decent job without having much skill. They really do boost your confidence! The drawing below was done in my first year – go ahead and copy it, I'll bet you do as good a job or better.

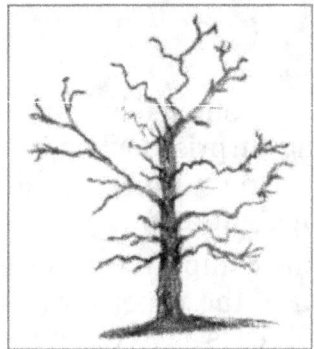

This type of artwork is so easy yet it looks smart and, you may have already guessed, I'm quite partial to it.

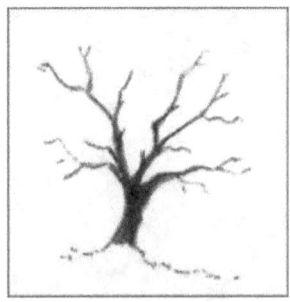

27 - COMPOSITION

After completing all the exercises discussed previously, you gain the understanding of what various parts mean to a plant. Arranging a drawing (composition) is yet another skill that is learned over time. If you become mindful of it now, that awareness grows with you.

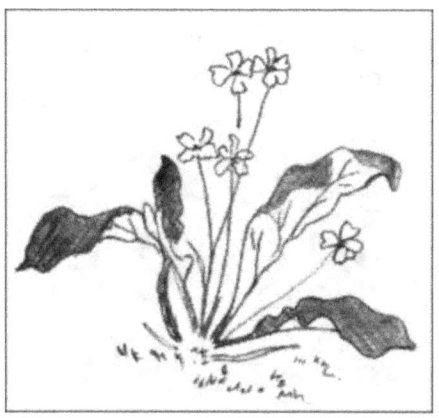

Just as different words are used in a story, you also need to make an interesting image by finding several forms and injecting a variety of tones (light and dark) into your sketch.

Composition means putting several things together to make one picture out of them. Each piece contributes towards a whole and it should be made as simple as possible.

Remember, this isn't anything you need to worry about right now but the following tips will help eventually with designing artwork.

In composition, unity comes first and the interdependence of composite parts comes second.

This book concentrates on very simple or single images so the following examples show good composition for those, along with some examples of what to avoid.

Overleaf, #1 isn't appealing because the line of growth is out of harmony with the border lines.

#2 is better because the border is adapted to the general shape and size of the spray. Even the vertical placement of initials keeps everything in harmony.

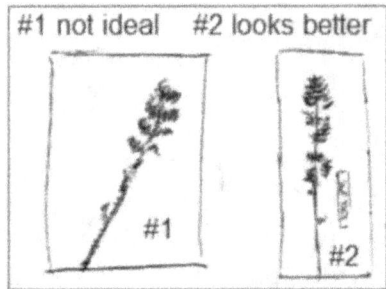

These images aren't distinct because their sole purpose is to show layout. Actually, they are scribbled in pen which is a great way to do quick thumbnail sketches.

#1 below isn't ideal with one spray sprawled over the sheet, making strong, oblique lines out of harmony to each other as well as the sides of the paper.

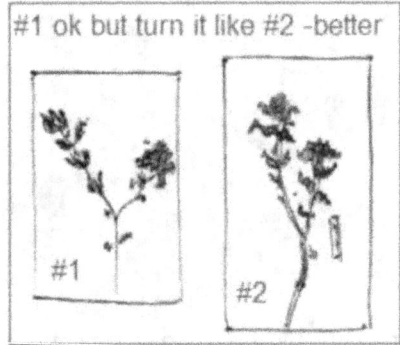

In #2, the same plant is turned so that the two heads form practically one mass, instantly making it more attractive.

Below, the one on the left isn't ideal for framing because interest is scattered. The line and angles of the stem tend to lead the eye away from the center and dissipates attention.

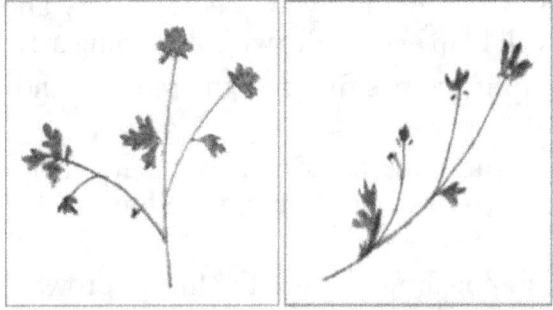

In the second one, the same sprig was turned to make the appearance a more compact whole. One flower is most prominent, while all others are smaller and their diminishing size still captivates. Some bits were omitted to make it more appealing.

A sketch of trees, arranged like those in the example below, has about the same effect on your audience as hitting one monotonous chord on a piano.

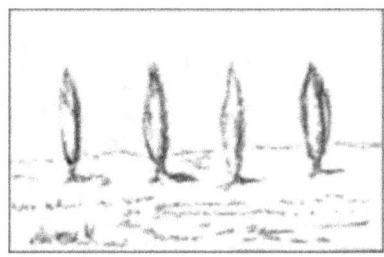

I'm guilty of doing sketches like this but once I learned about composition, I became more conscious about the outcome of my images.

Small rough sketches help you decide which layout is the most appealing. By studying them, you discover the easiest and most promising aspects.

In the next illustration, notice how the leaves are varied in size and position, how the stem changes its direction, how the berries grow, and how much more interesting it is rather than the repetition of the same leaf.

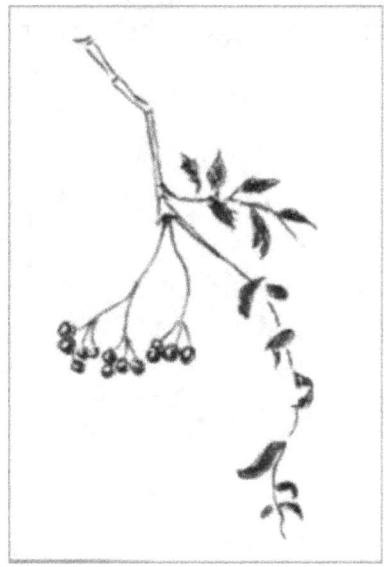

Let's do a flower that has pad-like leaves. This particular flower grows in an erratic way and the stems go everywhere. Here is the initial rough sketch...

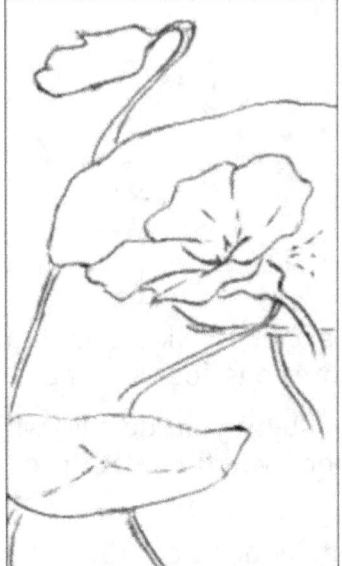

It doesn't seem to have any harmony but if I use my 'artistic license' to obtain unity, I can sketch in different lines while keeping in mind the range of possible growth. When I change it, I make sure the stems are placed so they appear unified and give a better appearance.

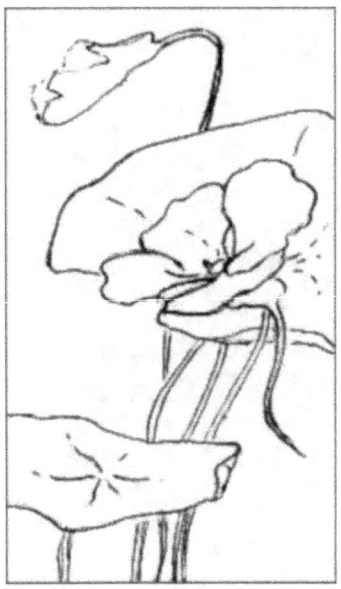

It pays to look for the general upward-and-outward tendency in each and every line or find a characteristic (familiar) curve repeated and echoed throughout. With practice, you achieve a gentle flow of shape into shape, the continuation of line and the subtlety of beautiful proportions.

You are able to use this artistic license to re-design in order to capture the typical beauty of a scene. You are the one who decides what is important in an image and how to express that importance.

In the image below, no enclosing line or border is used (the lines in this illustration represent the edges of the paper), so it suggests that the spray is a part of a larger, living whole. By making the stem diminish gradually, it looks like it disappears into the paper.

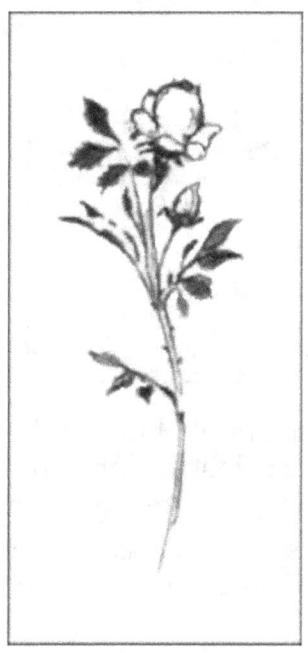

As the artist, you choose the center of interest. This is done by increasing detail in a selected part or by omitting detail. Unity, that all-important element of beauty, is obtained by emphasis.

You are like a photographer where you aim to capture the most pleasant facet of your subject. Choose a specimen and try different positions to select the best profile. If you are sketching from cut flowers, keep turning them to decide the finest angle to portray.

To emphasize something in a sketch, make the surroundings very plain or put less pressure on the pencil for the remainder of the sketch.

Sketching is different to drawing because a sketch is free and created in moments whereas a drawing takes longer with careful detail.

Sketch or draw with freedom and your skills automatically develop. You learn to draw by drawing so keep going one step at a time towards your ultimate achievement.

28 - DRAWING TIPS – BOOK 4

INTRODUCTION

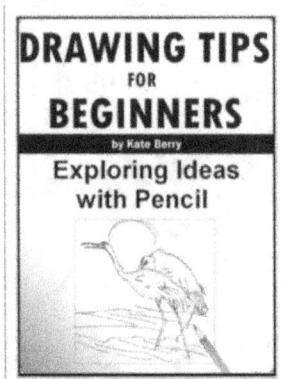

This section contains some simple but exciting pencil drawing tips that follow on from previous basic instruction. Now you are ready to progress on to the next (wonderful) stage of creating interesting drawings.

The following techniques really helped me achieve my goal to draw with confidence. It is now my privilege to have the opportunity to pass them on to you.

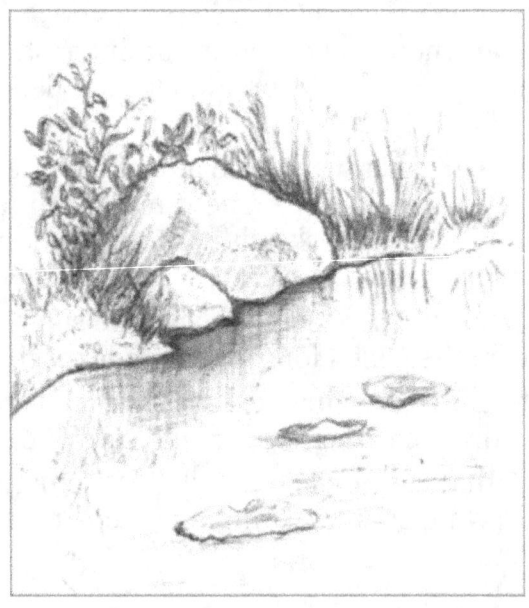

I don't profess to be an expert artist; in fact, I'm content to say I'm still learning. Drawing is a hobby that continuously offers challenges so it's pretty much a life adventure.

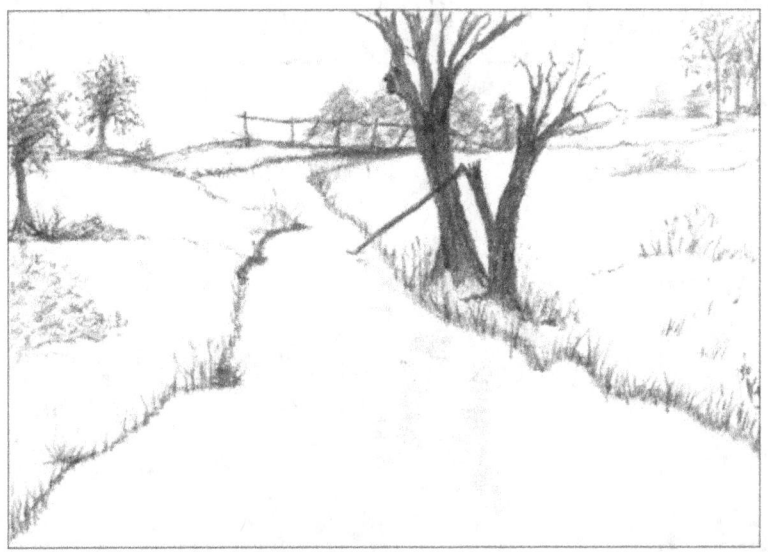

The images in this book are examples of my own work done at the time of practice, experimenting or when I was trying to do my best, so none are tidied up or made to look perfect. I make no excuses but I hope you're inspired to do better than this or at least see what's possible when you put in a little bit of effort.

On the upside, the fact that I am a mere hobby artist means I can introduce you to the real pleasure of drawing without overloading you with technical information or rules.

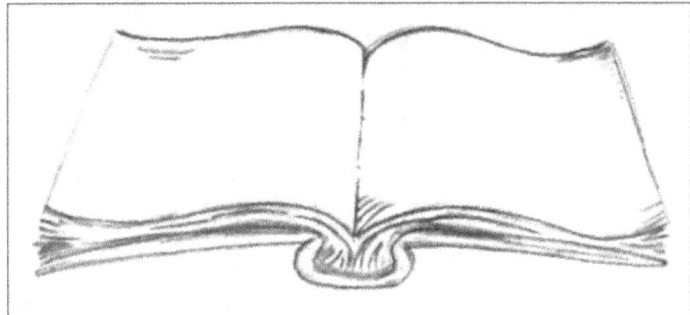

Believe me, I had a lot of crisis moments worrying if I should be writing books on this subject but I eventually decided that every single one of us knows something that we can share with someone else. Even if you learn only one little thing from these tips, it might just be the piece to the puzzle you were missing.

Before you start learning to draw, make sure you have the right mindset because your thought process does determine your success. If you're certain you'll never be able to draw, then I'm sad to say that's probably the way it will always be. You learned how to doubt yourself so why not learn how to believe in yourself? If you just try with patience and persistence, then your pencil will soon glide over the paper effortlessly. That might sound far-fetched but I promise it's true because I discovered it for myself.

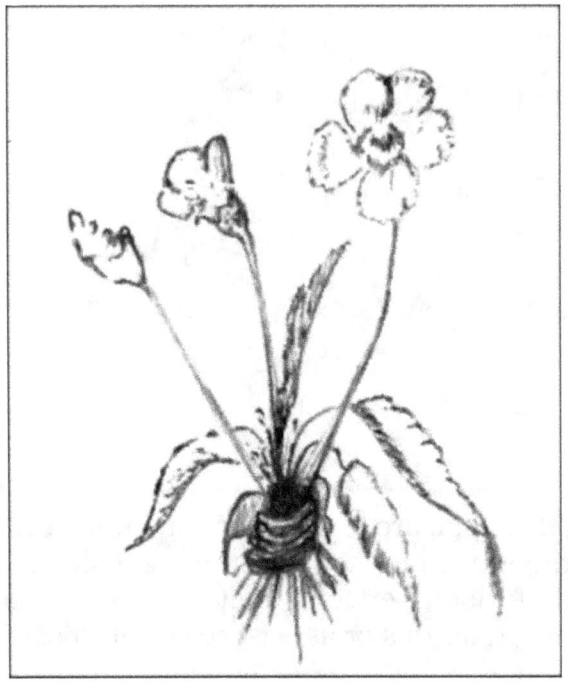

I was never a confident person but I was very keen to learn to draw. I adopted the attitude to give it my best shot (what did I have to lose?) and I'm sure that helped tremendously. So yes, you really need to believe in yourself.

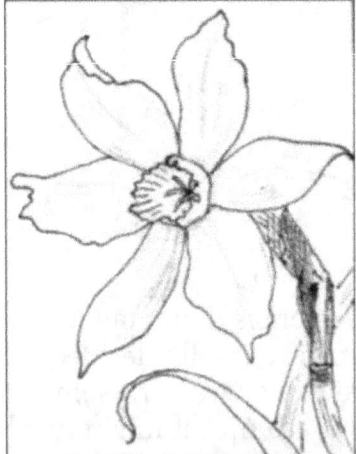

Another important thing I learned is not to waste time looking around for some kind of validation because if you don't have that inner belief to start with, you will never be convinced otherwise, no matter what kind of praise you receive.

It's only when you finally realize that you don't need anyone else's approval that all sorts of incredible things start to happen. So, focus only on what you want to achieve and you'll get there in quick time.

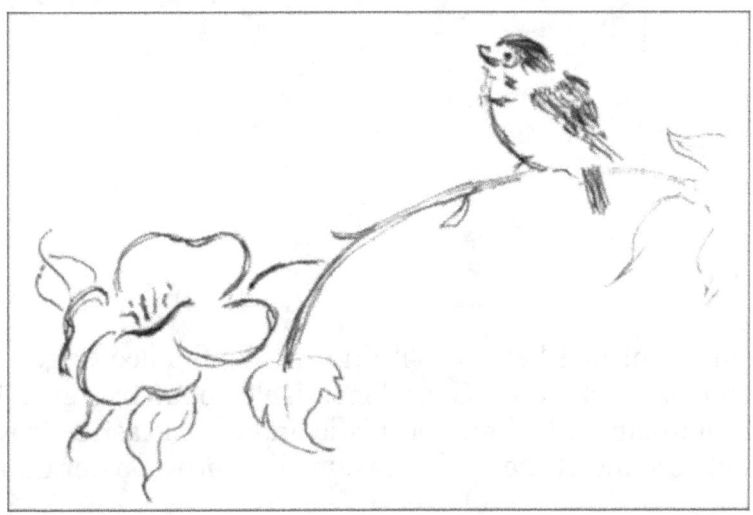

Ok, that's the pep talk over, let's move on...

The previous chapters in this "Teach Yourself To Draw" series are designed to help you create basic drawings.

Once that instruction is absorbed, it's normal to be in a state of not knowing what to do next. How do you advance and improve from this point? The bridge from that uncertain place to one of knowing can be summed up with one word and that is --- practice. It sounds like a long road, doesn't it?

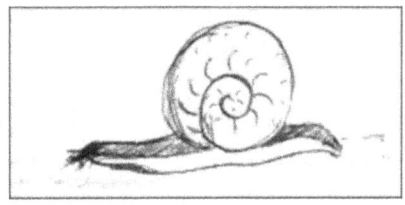

When I first started, the thought of practice represented a huge challenge, so I decided to look for ways to change the whole process into one of fun. It's so fortunate that we're not restricted to one rigid method to learn how to draw!

This tactic worked a treat so the following pages contain the many shortcuts that I feel propelled me along quickly. Simply by exploring and playing with these different ideas and suggestions, your improvement will be consistent, painless and totally enjoyable.

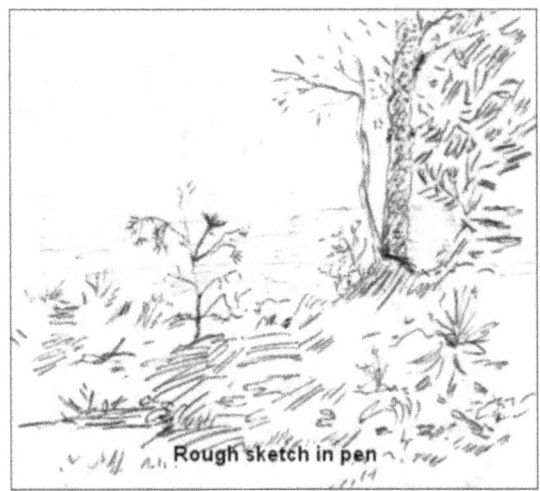

Rough sketch in pen

When you're finished here, you'll find the confidence to go on without being dependent on anyone. Confidence isn't about bragging how good you are, it's more about feeling optimistic and enthusiastic. Providing you actually practice some of these ideas, you will improve faster than you ever imagined.

A 2B wooden or mechanical pencil is used in most images in this book because 2B allows for dark or light lines (depending on pressure exerted) when needed. It's the most versatile grade of pencil and perfect for beginner artists. Whenever there is a different or additional pencil used, that information is provided along with the relevant drawing.

Pen is a good choice when doodling because it's usually close at hand. I did the next drawing while on the phone one day. It mainly consists of dots with an odd line here or there.

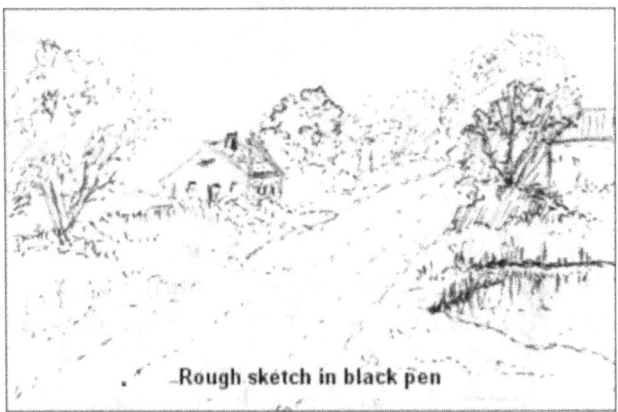

Rough sketch in black pen

Discovering which is your favorite pencil and paper is a fun exercise that could take a while but there's no hurry, generally any pencil and paper will do for most purposes.

29 - FINDING THE ZONE

To draw productively, we need to access a certain part of the brain. I won't go into detail about the complexity of the human brain but what it basically means is the lesser-used right side of the brain is available to us for creative work. The dominating left side keeps us on our toes for most of the day and it's just not beneficial for drawing.

There are a few different ways to tune into the right side but I find the easiest is to <u>draw with the hand you don't normally use</u>. As soon as the analytical (left) brain detects awkward movement and can't work out what's going on, it hands over the task to the creative (right) side and you then become in "the zone".

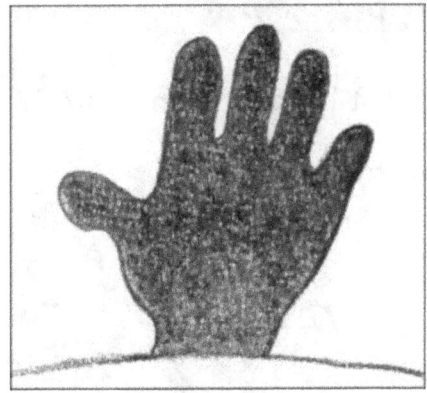

Now, here's the tricky part... unless you're ambidextrous, it's going to be a struggle to hold onto the pencil let alone try to draw something!

My advice is to grab the pencil as best as you can and immediately draw a line, any length, in any direction. Once you do that, a switch occurs over to the creative side and it so happens you're no longer bothered about how to hold the pencil. Your main focus becomes drawing and not your grip.

The following photos show how I hold a pencil but you will find your own way, just do it however it comes – you'll realize once you start that nothing matters anyway.

Below - Side grip for loose work with left (non-dominant) hand:

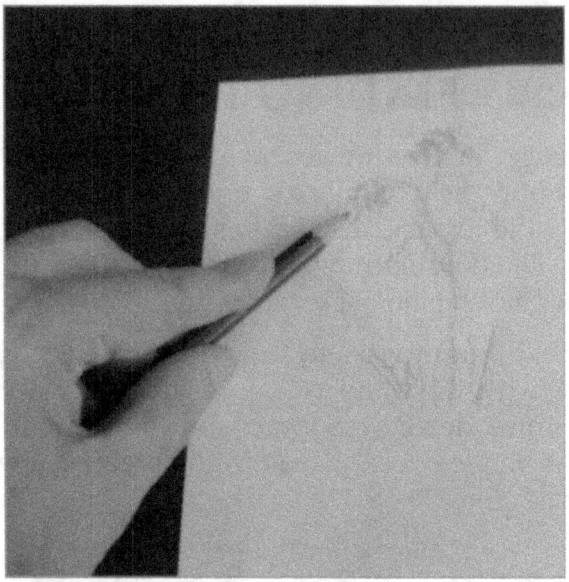

Below - Writing grip (left-handed) for finer work:

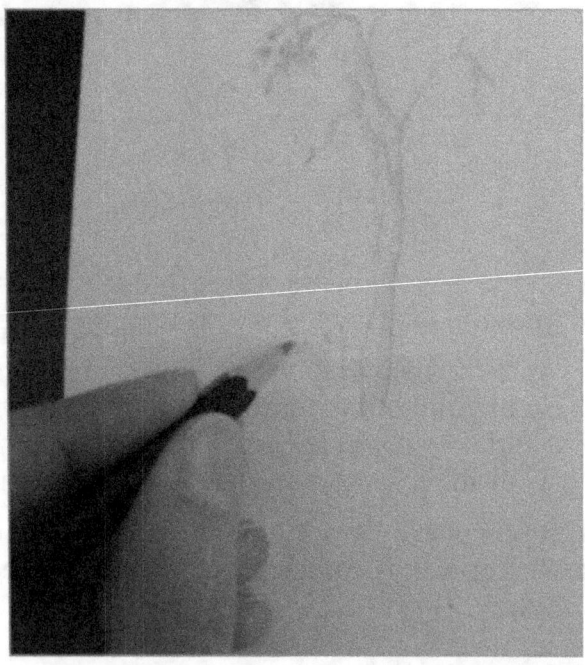

If you like a challenge, have a pencil in each hand to simultaneously draw basic shapes like triangles, squares and circles. Shapes are symmetrical (two halves identical) and perfect for two-hand exercises.

This is called ambidextrous drawing and it co-ordinates the two hands so they work together freely and harmoniously. With only a little practice, you soon develop skill, freedom, and speed. Don't worry about accuracy; the idea is to improve through repetition while the hand and mind learn how to work together.

Draw whatever you wish, there's no set pattern to follow so just make it up as you go along.

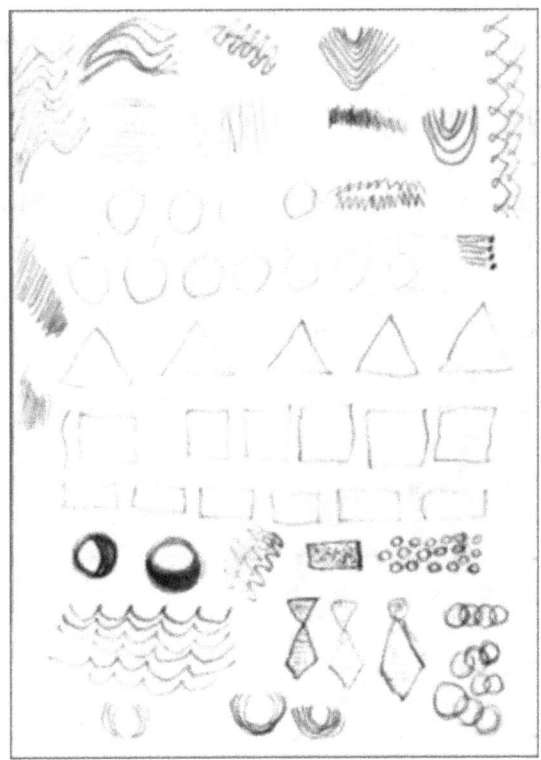

Once you're totally absorbed drawing left-handed, you go on to produce all sorts of images.

Let your intuition guide you at this point but I was compelled to draw a great variety of subjects as shown in the following examples. It really is astounding to witness - it's like you're a third party looking on and the outside world just fades away.

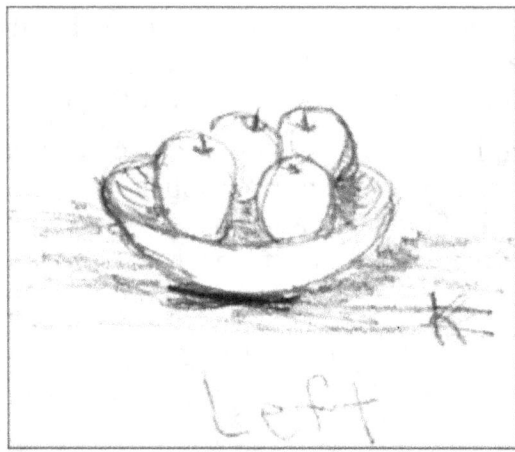

It's a liberating feeling to have no expectations and every single image makes you question that if you can produce reasonable artwork with your non-dominant hand, what are you really capable of producing with your favored hand?

That's why this is a great exercise, it clearly demonstrates you can achieve drawings that your mind usually tells you that you can't do!

My go-to left hand exercise is always landscape because nature can be portrayed in so many ways. I enjoy sketches and using my left hand shows me how to reduce images to the barest essentials. One great advantage is that you definitely learn how to let go of fussiness.

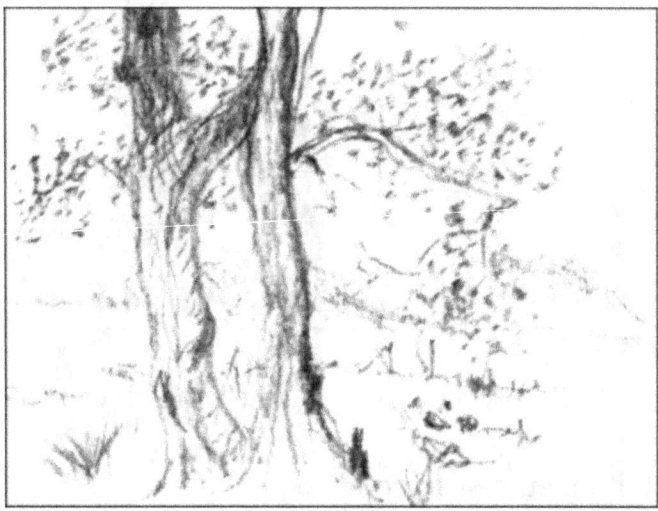

If you review your drawings at a later date and feel inclined to make adjustments, make sure you use the same awkward (non-dominant) hand otherwise the thrill of that creation is lost.

It doesn't matter if lines don't go the way you want them to, don't erase but continue adding more lines until it feels and looks right. Creations like this have spirit and personality.

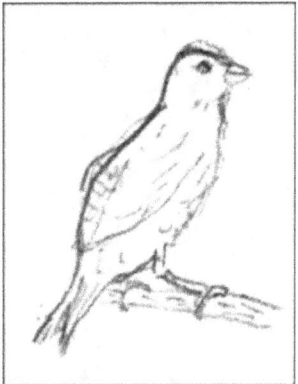

The next drawing isn't my best left-handed work but it's a good example showing how I tried to find the right lines :)

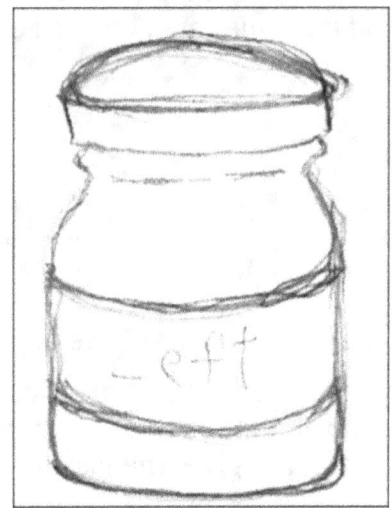

I hold my pencil in a writing grip for lines (left-handed) but, once again, that's a personal choice.

Using the opposite hand teaches us many things but the main lesson is that anything is possible if you try -- the proof is right there in front of you.

I encourage you to try this particular exercise at least once because the benefits far outweigh any reluctance you may feel. With each session, you become more familiar with holding and using the pencil in this fashion.

I keep a separate sketchbook for my left hand drawings and I still marvel at the images created in this way. As usual, always date your work and make any notes you feel are relevant to each image.

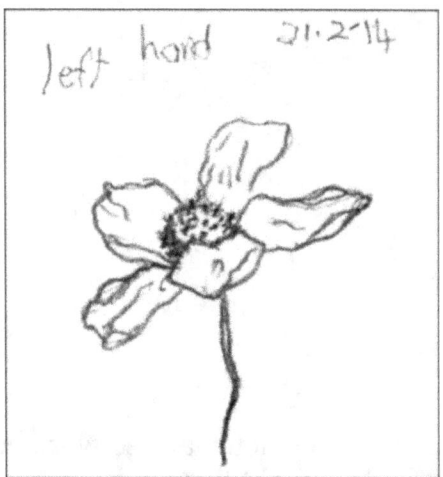

I enjoy thumbnail drawing so doing them with my left hand was interesting -- the following examples are actual size.

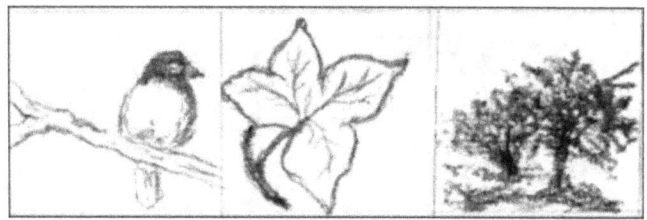

You'll learn more about thumbnail drawings in Chapter 36.

There are lots of ways to get into the zone (accessing the right side of the brain). Another popular method is to copy an upside down picture but in my opinion, using the left hand gives the fastest results.

You now have an excuse to produce untidy, unappealing images and believe me, that's the best thing that can ever happen to any beginner artist. Be prepared to surprise yourself!

Personally, I think this exercise helps you tap into your unlimited potential which paves the way towards a brighter artistic future.

30 - VISUALIZATION

Long before I ever thought I could draw, I used to examine faces and mentally draw them. It was this consistent habit that finally motivated me to teach myself to draw.

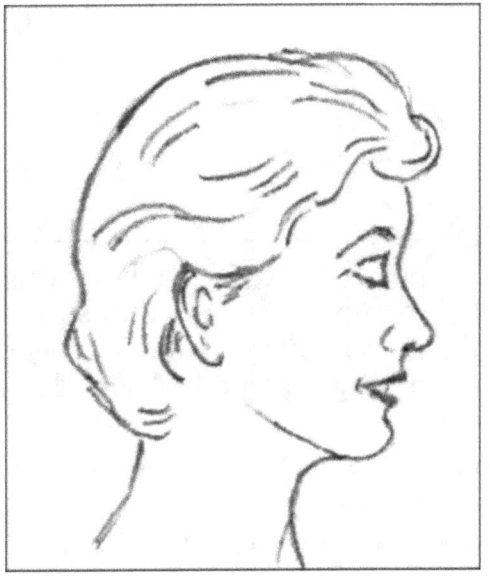

I didn't realize it at the time, but the habit of visualizing propelled me forward faster by covertly improving my observation skills, making learning to draw a much easier task.

Pick any subject/object to study and imagine how you'd create a similar form. I usually begin by following the outline (outside area) using my eyes as an imaginary pencil.

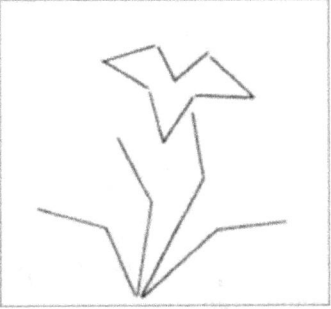

There are many ways to visualize and I really don't want to influence you with one set method because you will automatically find what suits you. I simply share what I do as a form of guidance but ultimately the choice is always yours -- this is your adventure.

Let's use a straight glass as the first example. With your eyes, follow the vertical lines and curves that form the whole shape. Notice there are no horizontal lines in the formation.

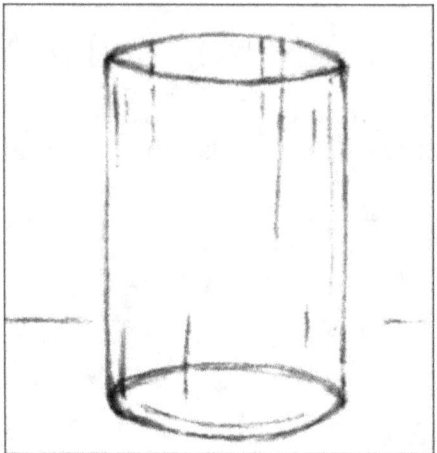

When you make a point of observing lines (horizontal, vertical or angled) in all objects, it occupies your mind in such a way that you don't even think to name the items. You see, when we identify things, our mind tries to dominate how an image should look and that means we don't end up with a true portrayal.

Mental drawing teaches you to observe the way an artist does and that is purely by line, shape and color.

Angled lines are sometimes very slight so use your finger to judge and compare the variation.

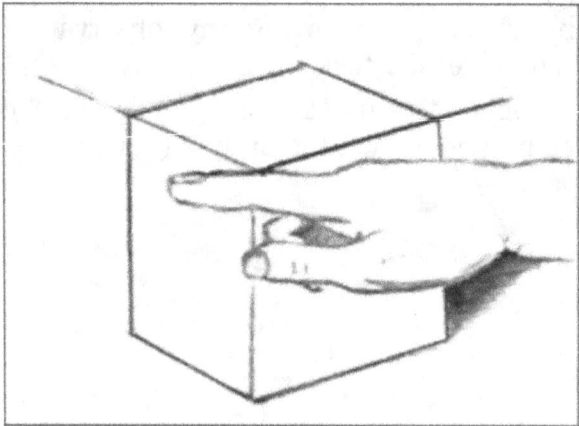

Of course, you can use a pencil (or whatever) but when you're visualizing, that's not always convenient.

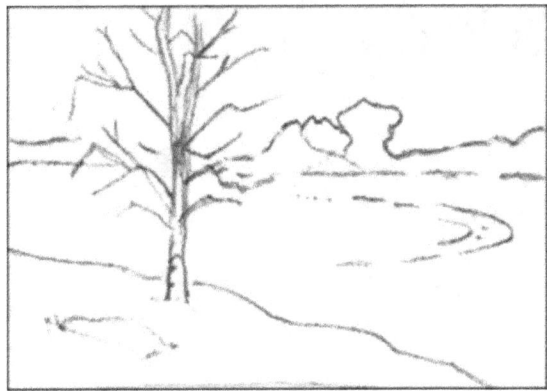

For landscapes, the idea is to mentally form a type of skeleton using only the main objects that make up a scene.

This is a skeleton:

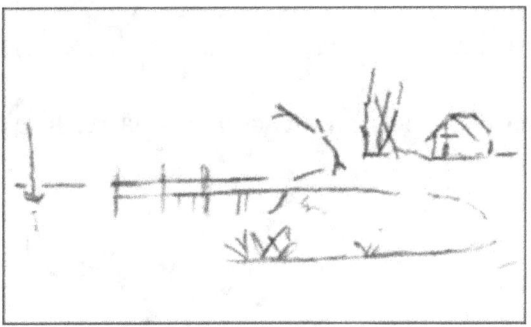

of this:

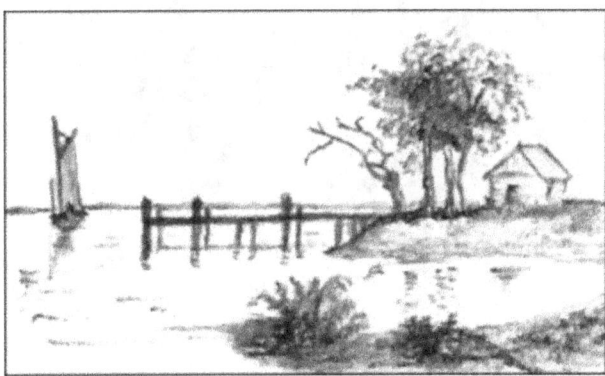

The process is similar to creating a bare-boned outline that you might first pencil in if you were drawing on paper but for now, we're creating these skeleton outlines in our minds.

Here is another skeleton...

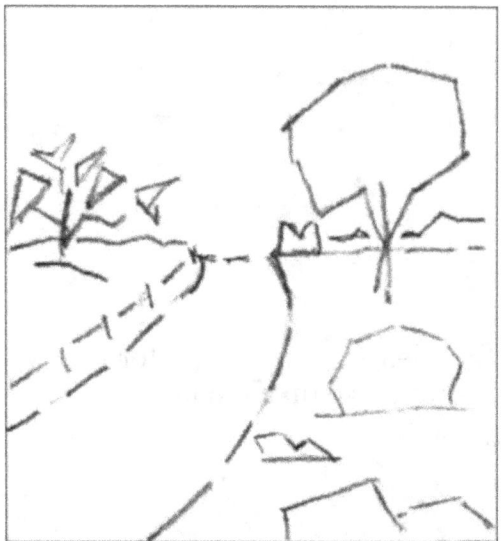

that can later be developed into a scene on paper like this...

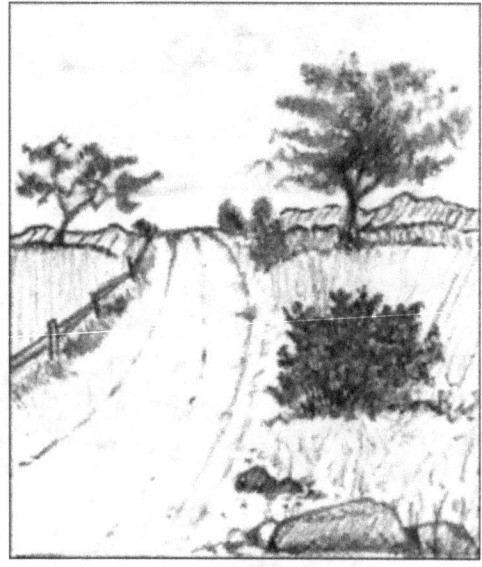

Another very beneficial visualizing project is to identify shapes (squares, circles, triangles, etc.) within your chosen subject. To use a cat as an example, a circle represents the head and an oval for the body so you might roughly sketch in those shapes to get first impressions.

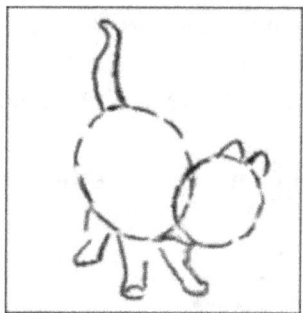

There are lots of animals to study this way; for example, a chick can be constructed by merging 2 circles...

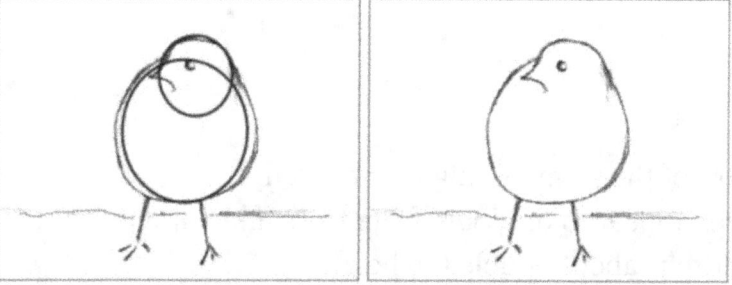

My most regular visualizing session is done when I look out the window (day dreaming) and mentally draw the tree across the road. It's great practice studying how branches shoot out from the trunk and to observe main lines that form the overall shape. I do this so often, I'm sure I'd recognize that tree if it was ever moved to another location!

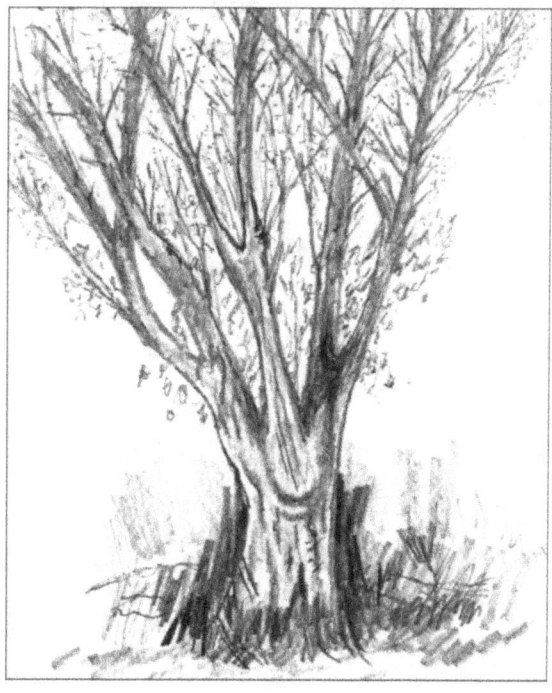

By studying or visualizing trees beforehand, you learn the general character of each type. Remember, you don't have to portray trees exactly or even know the genre; you only need the perception of how it appears to you.

Now let's study a snippet of nature together using this image...

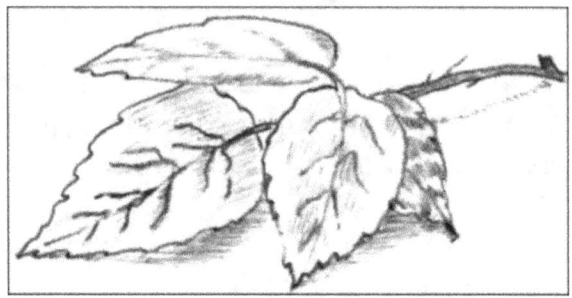

Observe:

** the flow of the stem - straight or curved.

** 3 leaves appear to originate from the same point on the stem.

** the width is about double the height.

** the stem is barren of leaves for about one third of the length.

** shapes of leaves.

** where shadow falls.

Just by doing this, you create a habit of noticing important points of interest and that information is automatically considered in your next drawing. It's like a flow-on effect of study and implementation.

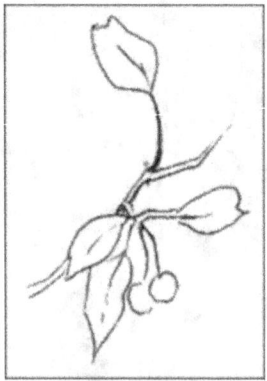

If portraits are what you want to specialize in, start the learning process with profiles because that is the easiest aspect of a face. It's a good visualization exercise to follow the contour and notice which part protrudes further than the rest and which part is indented the most.

Make silent observations about the shape of a forehead or eyebrows, notice how the ear sits roughly between the eye and the nose and keep doing this type of study while mentally drawing at the same time.

As part of your visual study of faces, make a habit of comparing the size of the eye to every other feature. All tutorials for portrait and anatomy drawing involve comparisons, measuring and guidelines of one part to another. This visualization technique builds a good foundation for whenever you dedicate the time to studying and drawing the human form.

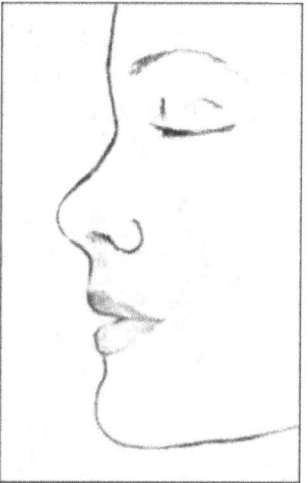

I probably need to mention that drawing people is one of the hardest subjects and even now I can't say I do it well! It's a process for me, some turn out really good and others, well, let's just say they existed for the greater good :)

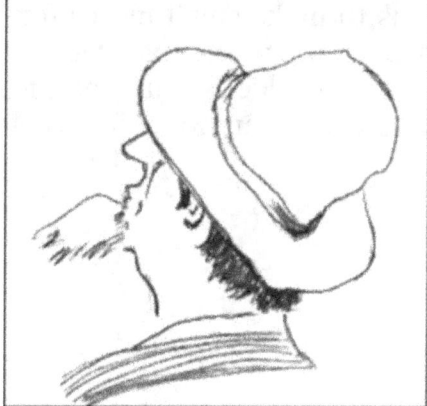

Last of all, I'd like to mention the one thing that used to really intimidate me was the constant reminder to draw everyday otherwise I won't retain the skill. Life is busy so it's not always possible to find time to draw but by drawing mentally, my progression continues, albeit in a different way.

Learning by doing is definitely the way to go but if you don't get a lot of time to draw, visualizing is the next best thing!

31 - MEASURING TIPS

Beginners are usually over-eager to draw subjects that are beyond their level of ability and disappointment at an early stage is very discouraging. With this next tip, a trainee can now successfully draw a good variety of subjects while still developing practical skills.

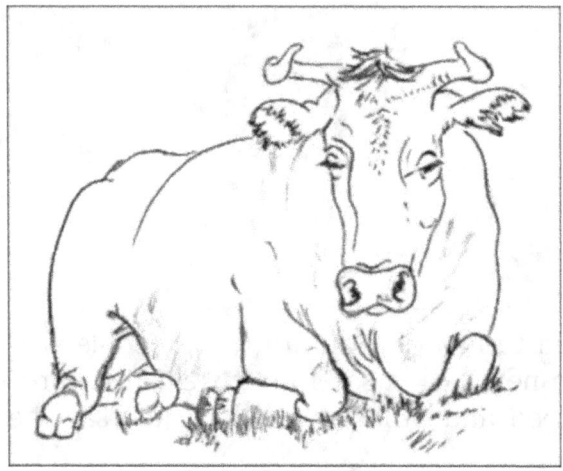

The general concept is to make small marks for height and width of a particular subject or to just mark where major items sit within a picture. It depends on what picture you select so just look for the most prominent features to measure and make a mark for guidance.

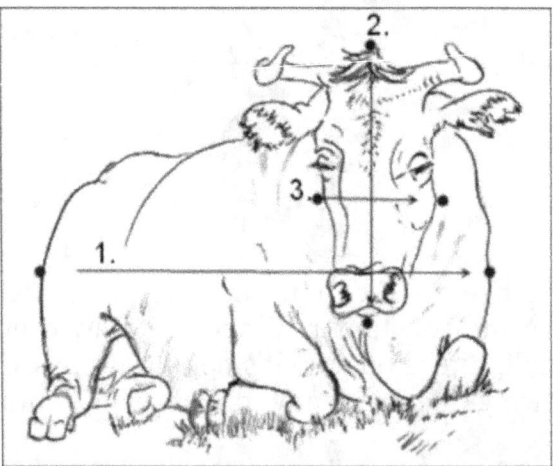

Proportion is hard to get right but once some markers are in place (as in 1 – 3 above), you have a basic idea of where things belong and the drawing evolves easily. The best way to learn this technique is to do it together, step by step, so please follow along...

First of all, it's your preference if you want to measure and rule up a border to the same dimensions of the picture you're copying. To make it simpler, an "L" shape can also be used to represent the left and bottom borders.

We're going to use a photo of a ceramic dog as the subject for our first practice session.

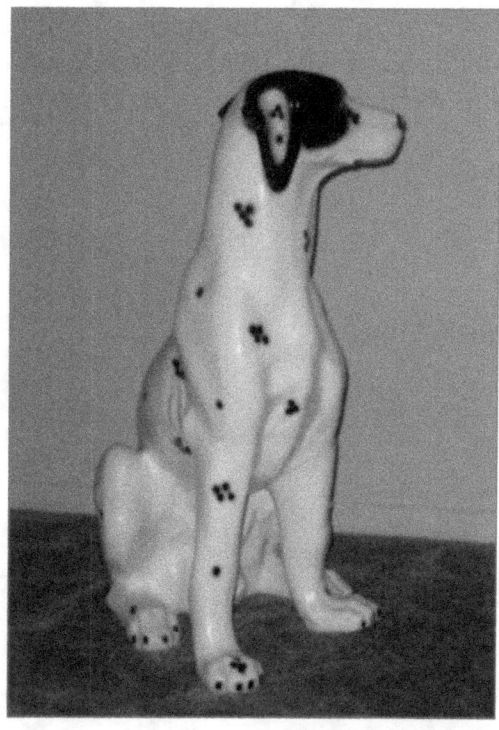

To start off, mark the height with a top and bottom marker, as well as the width of the head from tip of nose to back of head. Use your pencil as a ruler or use an actual ruler, it doesn't matter.

If you are keen to see what you can produce, here's your chance to sketch in the rest of the outline to the best of your ability. It's amazing how those few simple markers make the job so much easier, just by making you aware that you need to get it all in, in that space.

As you go along, make comparisons with every other part, for example, starting from the top and on the right...

1. The neck is just slightly behind the position of the eye (using an imaginary vertical line).

2. After the neck is in place, the line slants out but stay aware that the leg doesn't protrude past the widest point which is the nose.

3. Continue making this type of comparison until one side is completed and then use points along the finished portion to judge where the line varies on the other side.

Sometimes it helps to roughly measure different widths along the way, just to stay on track.

Remember to keep your initial lines light – in the drawing below, the lines are darkened for display. The best way to do an outline is to use all straight lines and later make adjustments where needed.

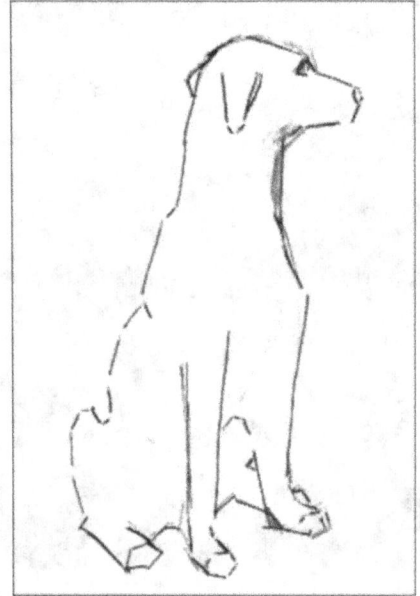

It's easier to judge placement of angled lines if the drawing paper is directly beneath the picture you want to copy. Copying from the computer is different but by referencing the picture continuously, it's still achievable.

When you've got a good blocked-in shape (compared with the original), proceed to lightly adjust the lines to properly follow the form.

If the drawing doesn't look right, go back and do some measuring comparisons for a quick fix.

After making adjustments, darken the outline to finish. Remember, your drawing doesn't have to be exactly right – if you want perfection, you can trace it but that's not near as much fun, is it?

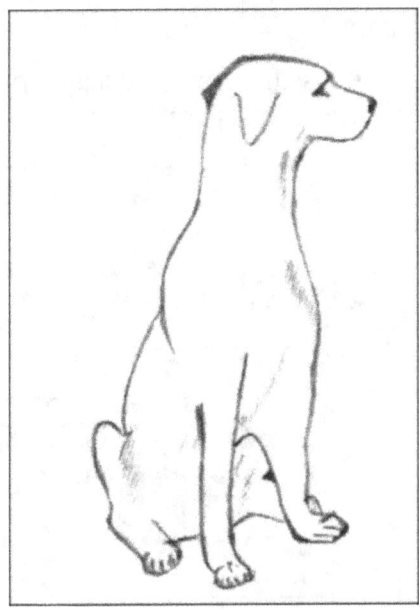

With only a couple of markers here and there, you basically do this drawing on your own and that's all the encouragement you need to keep going! You CAN draw, you just have to prove it to yourself first and this is one way to do that.

Below is another block-in example of the same subject from a slightly different angle.

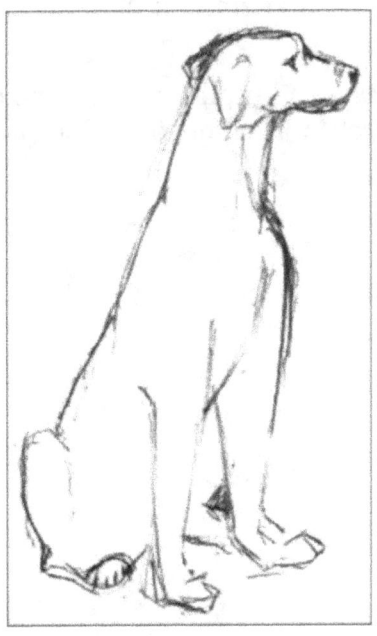

Using markers for landscapes:

Markers aren't really necessary for landscape but in the early stages, this little bit of guidance gives a lot of confidence to rookie artists.

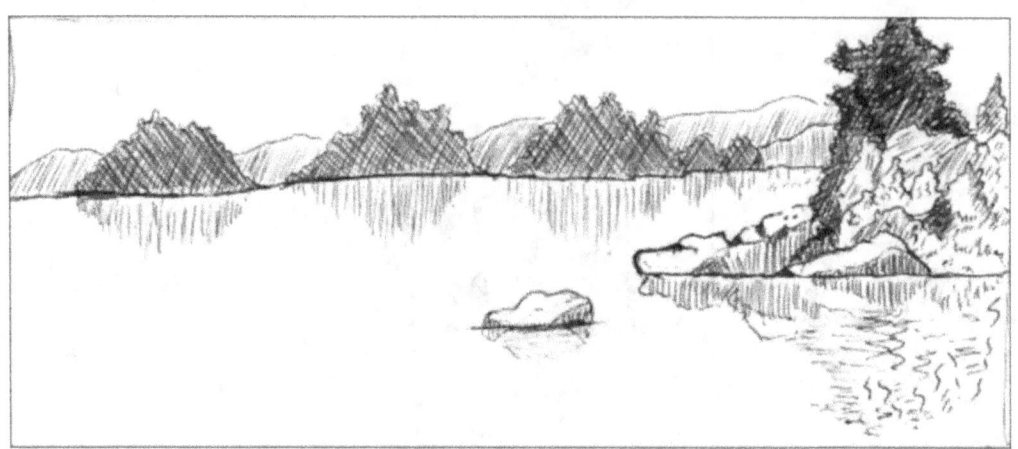

If you were to draw the landscape above, roughly measure and place marks to indicate where the rocks protrude from the right border as well as from the bottom border.

Next measure how high the land line (on the left) is from the bottom border. Place as many dots as you feel you need.

The single rock in the water can be judged by guessing, it's not imperative that it's exact, but keeping it close to land gives the impression of shallow water.

The shape and height of the mountains can be estimated by the size of the trees in front, so there's no real need to place markers for those.

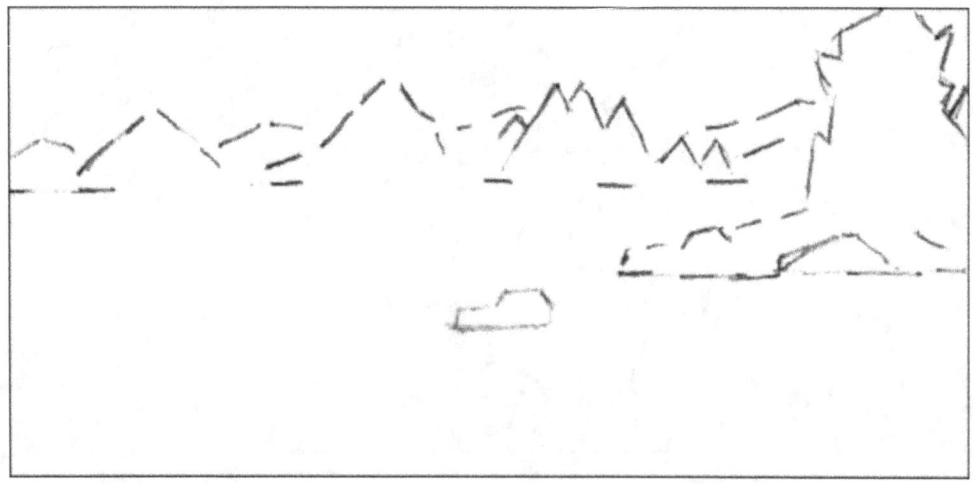

When you have a good idea where everything belongs, start creating a light outline with the help of the reference picture and the markers. Once the initial outline looks good, start darkening main lines and add shading.

For shading, the mountains are depicted with light diagonal lines going in one direction only because they're in the background and should appear indistinct.

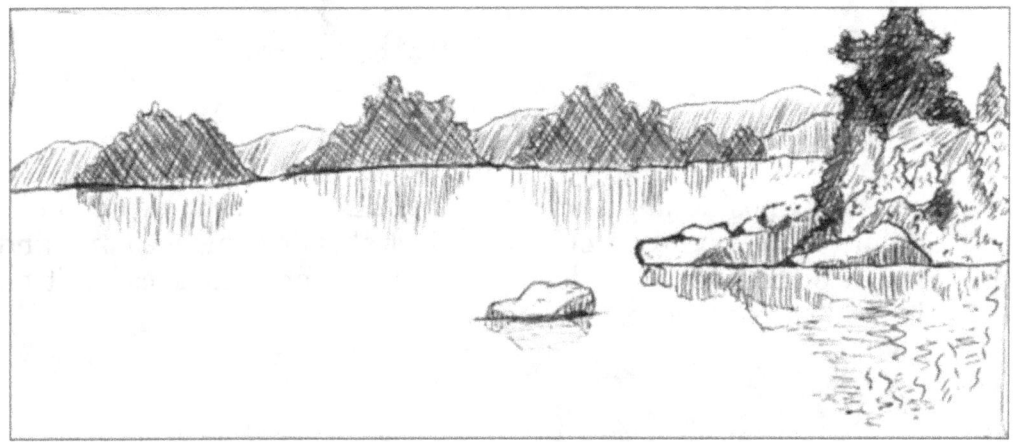

The trees in front of the mountain can be a bit darker because they're nearer, so a cross hatch does that job by angling lines one way and then reversing them.

Naturally, you still make the usual observations to create an image:-

1. Estimating angles

2. Comparing size of one object to next (proportion)

3. Judging light and dark areas.

Now you have an idea of why I love landscapes -- being shown how to depict things in a simple way makes all the difference. You may not need this type of instruction but we're all at different stages of learning and it could be helpful to someone. I never thought I'd be able to translate a photo into a drawing but it happened naturally after practicing with measure markers.

When teaching yourself to draw, there are many shortcuts that help you achieve a good likeness. You can't draw like an expert immediately, it's a gradual process, so these tricks are simply like training wheels that give you a great deal of satisfaction from your artwork. You won't always rely on them but they sure do help you gain experience and confidence along the way.

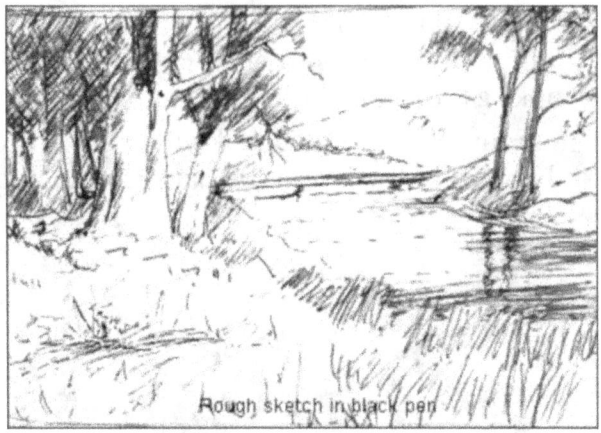

You can apply positioning marks to many subjects but it isn't suitable for everything so if you ever feel hassled, just abandon this idea and find something else that works. It doesn't hurt to experiment because it all results in productive practice.

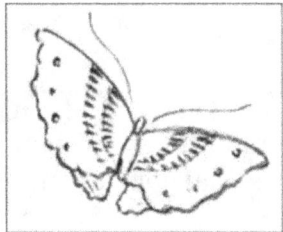

Once you're comfortable with measuring and marking from pictures, it's a natural transition towards getting correct proportions when you draw from life.

You often see artists holding their pencil out in front of them with a straight arm and one eye closed. They are measuring their subject - height, width and estimating the size of one thing against another.

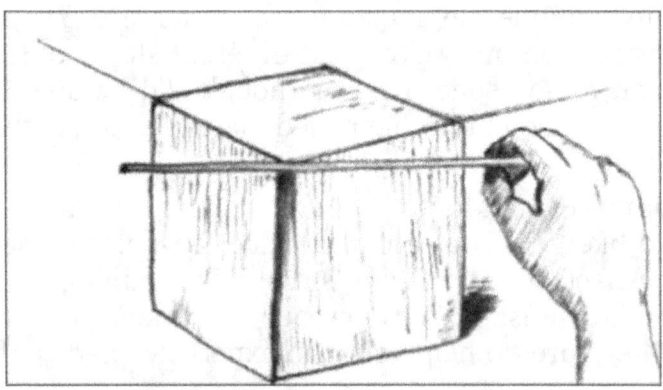

Most artists perform some type of measuring, so never feel reluctant to use whatever helps you get a good result.

If you draw a picture freehand (without any markers), it's good to revisit the drawing later and again compare it with the original. I usually discover my judgment isn't as good as I first thought but I make allowances for the experience.

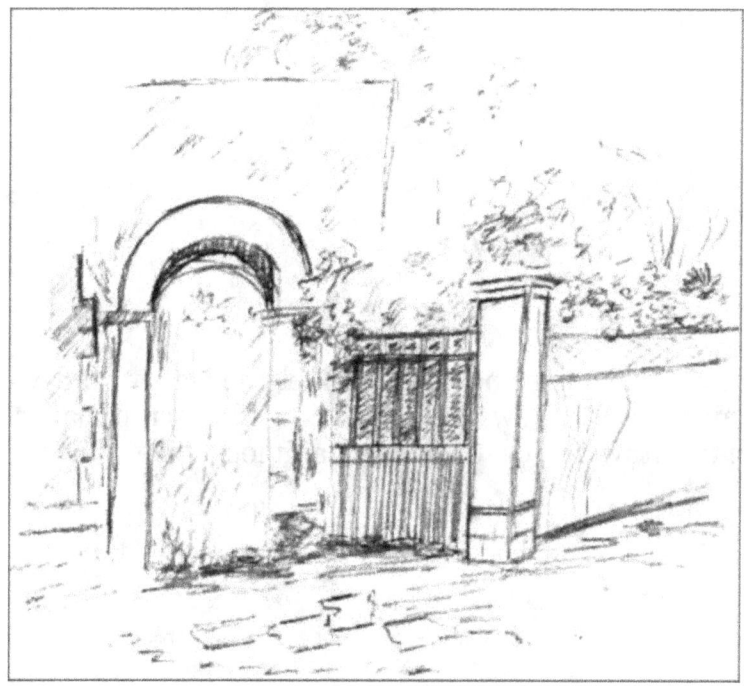

The sketch above was done freehand and while I like it, it wouldn't pass a test in art school!

Using Scrap Paper as a guide

You can use a scrap of paper for a measuring device (to assist with proportion) when copying from photos or pictures. This is mostly helpful when you draw a portrait or a busy picture like a landscape.

This particular method is just an alternative to using your pencil as a ruler.

The size or shape of the paper doesn't matter; it's only for a guide. You can select one item to compare the size of one thing against another or you can measure each individual item. The latter sounds like too much work for me but it might be of use to someone.

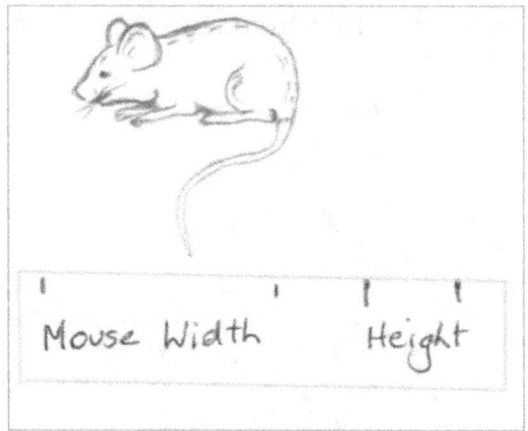

In the mouse drawing above, I marked the height and width of the mouse from a picture I wanted to copy. The scrap paper I used is underneath the drawing, just to show what it looks like.

In a landscape, a tree is a good item to use as a measuring guide.

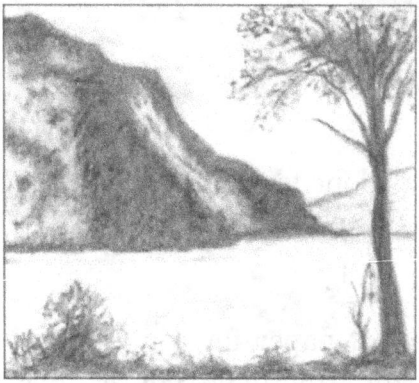

The act of first measuring the tree brings your attention to the landscape as a whole because you immediately notice that the tree is either higher or shorter than a building (or other point of interest) nearby. From there, everything else gets compared to the size of the tree.

It is by continually doing comparisons that all components fit nicely into a drawing and proportion takes care of itself.

32 - DRAWING FREEHAND

Each artist uses a different method to draw. For me, I like to continuously test myself to see what I can produce first without using any guidelines. I get mixed results but that's all part of the adventure.

If a subject looks a bit tougher than normal, I'm not too proud to use something like the measure method discussed in the previous chapter.

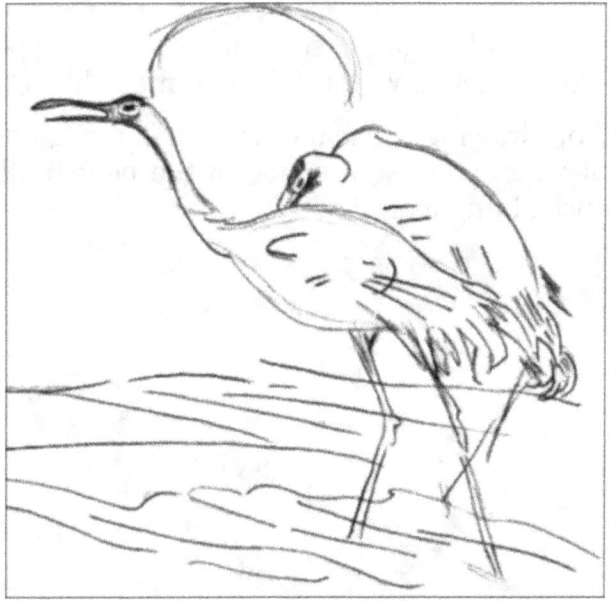

Whatever you draw, it's your impression of that scene or object. You draw differently to me and everyone else because we all see things in a unique way. Draw whatever you like and enjoy it without asking for someone's critique because that can zap all pleasure away from you instantly.

I learned that drawing with the side of a pencil gave me a freedom like I'd never experienced before so I insist you try it!

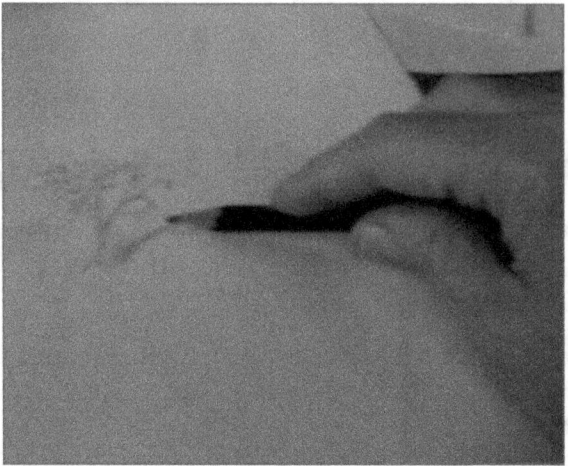

The photo above is only a guide; sometimes I grip the pencil nearer the end. Always hold the pencil however it feels comfortable to you.

The thought of drawing freehand can make beginner artists very apprehensive but when you use the side of the pencil, all inhibitions go away – miraculously, I might add!

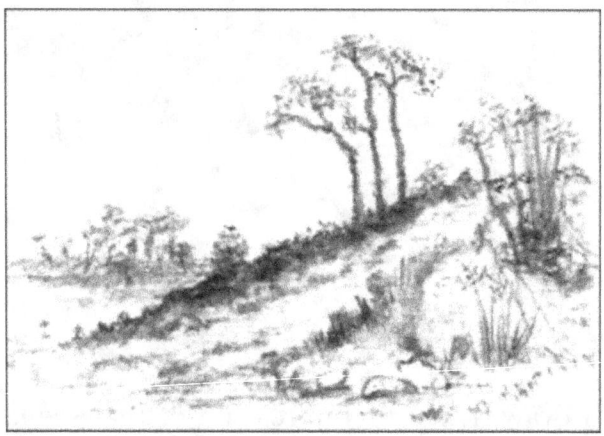

The sketch above is one of the first ones I did with the side of the pencil and I'll never forget my amazement at how effortlessly it evolved. It's sort of like a scribble with a hint of design - it's interesting to watch an image emerge.

Remember that progression is a gradual thing so always think simple and everything flows naturally. Another great learning exercise is to draw a subject at least twice.

I started the habit of re-doing basic images like this:

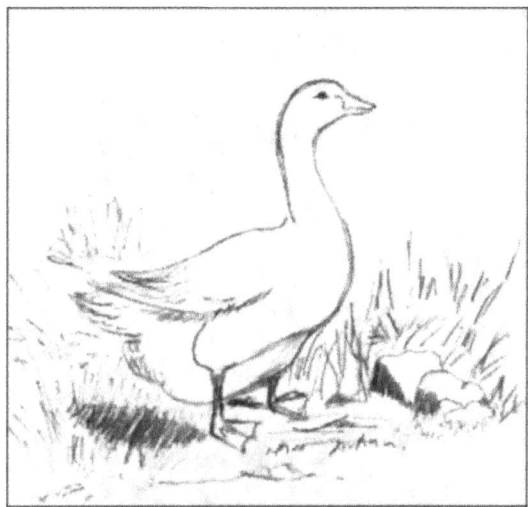

There's a lot to observe and even if you give it your full concentration and do a good job, it's when you re-draw it the second time that you realize what kind of detail slipped past your attention.

After following the 'start simple' approach, fast forward to now and I'm at the stage where I draw a lot of landscapes twice. Here's a photo of a pretty scene that I felt compelled to draw:

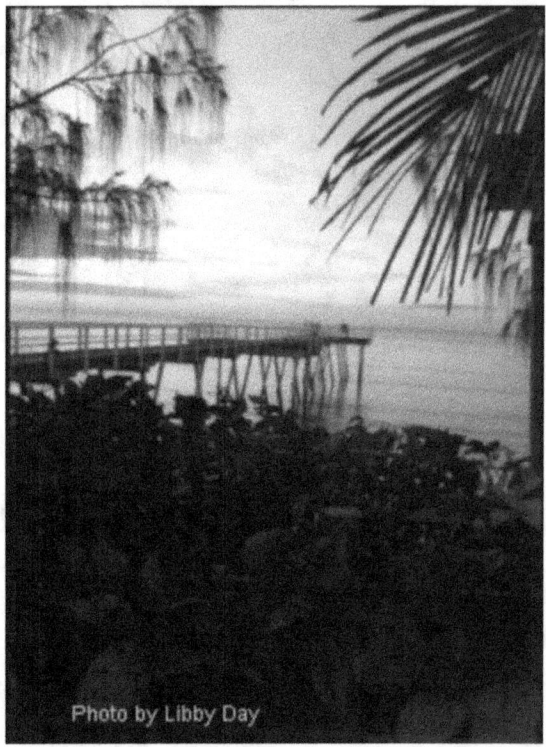

(Photo taken at Hervey Bay, Queensland, Australia)

I had a spare half hour so I was soon absorbed in drawing it. I became so involved I wasn't aware of the moment when I started fiddling and adding too many details, as shown in this illustration...

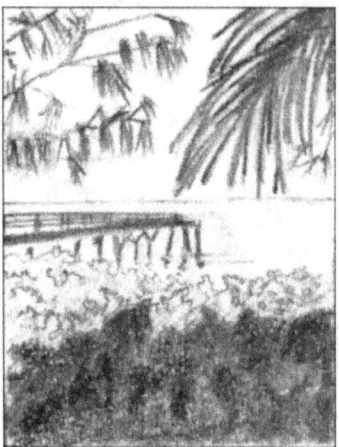

When I look at a drawing where I went overboard with detail, I resolve to roughly sketch the same scene again just to show myself how easy it can be without too much bother.

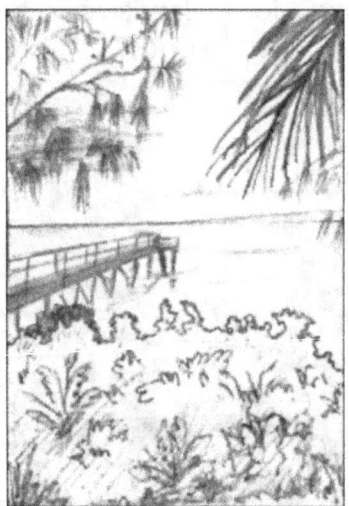

I am more observant the second time around. It really teaches me to pay attention to finer details like how the jetty isn't parallel to the horizon line (where ocean meets sky) which is a mistake I made in the first one. If I did a third drawing, I'd draw the jetty at an even finer angle to the horizon.

Of course, always refer to the original picture when you re-draw because you won't learn anything if you copy from your own work.

Here are more examples from another photo that I rendered - the first one was way too busy (in my opinion) and the second is a rough sketch.

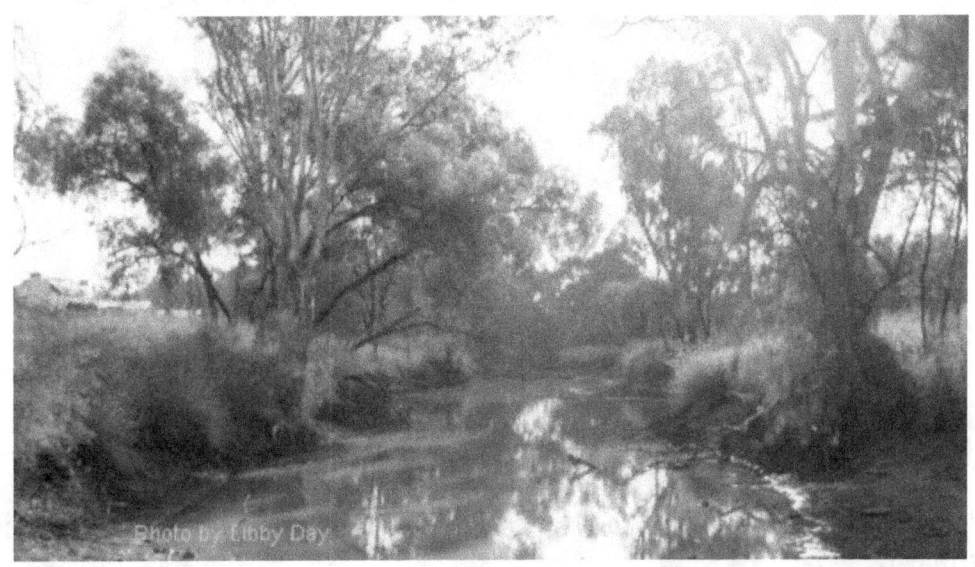

(Photo taken at Wallumbilla Creek, Queensland, Australia)

This is what happens when I become totally engrossed...

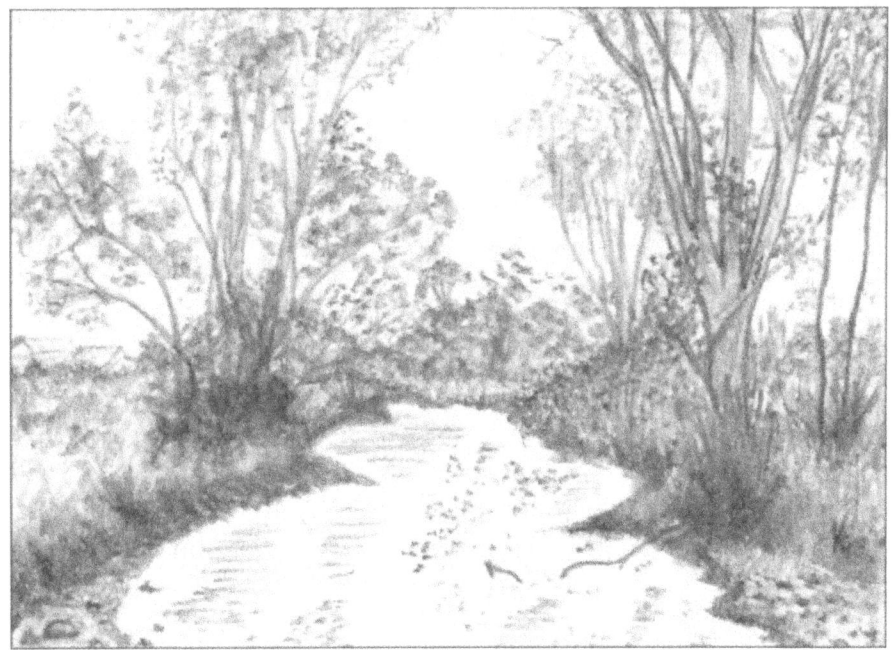

A quick sketch of the same scene...

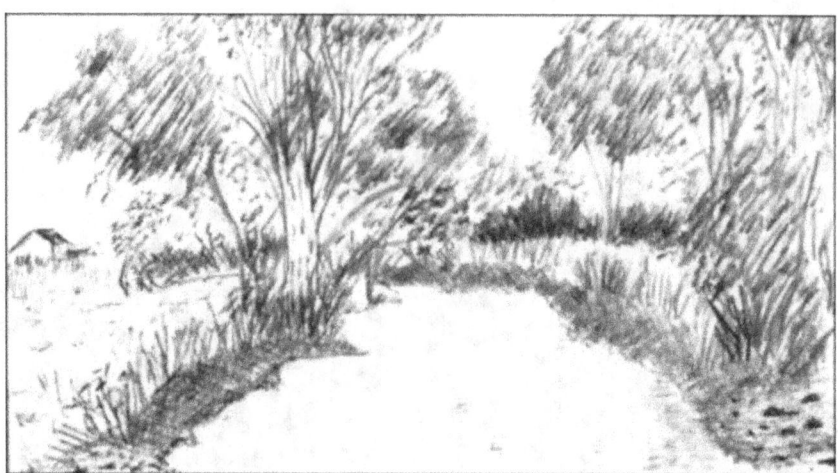

It continues to fascinate me how many different ways there are to depict a subject.

If you're not drawing the way you'd like, drawing the same subject more than once is something you need to try. All you have to do is resolve to do it differently and it will happen that way.

Please don't just read this advice, you have to try it out and make the discovery yourself -- you'll never forget the experience.

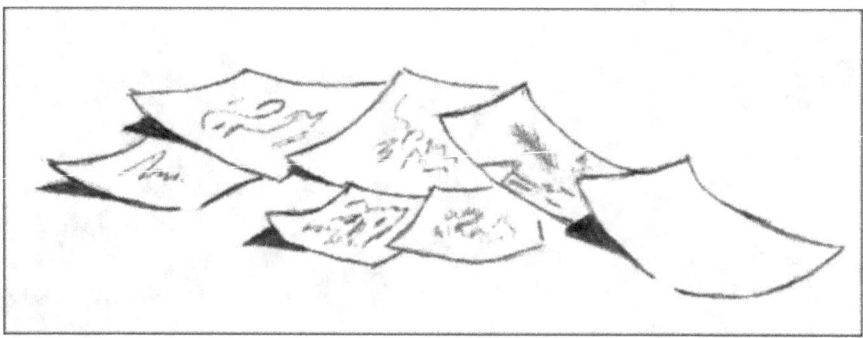

It's by this type of experimentation with different techniques that you ultimately find what you really prefer and you'll soon get into a nice routine.

Let's Scribble

Scribbling is a wonderful way to get used to drawing freehand. I love it because I give myself permission to create messy images and I don't care about the outcome. If you're a harsh self-critic, then this is for you!

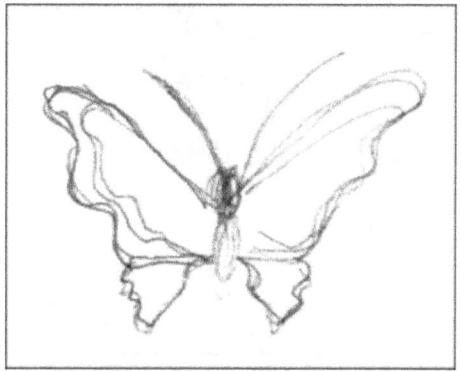

Sidebar

You might notice a theme of "giving permission" or "allowing" throughout this book but I think it's important. Too many of us are hung up on what people think and that's a complete waste of time. Life is too short for worrying about "what if" scenarios. I don't care what anyone thinks of my drawings, everyone has an opinion but I don't have to ask for it or hear it. My main aim is to help you be the best you can be and if that means showing my learner drawings then I'm up for it!

End sidebar

Scribbling helps you to find the feel of a subject and that knowledge is automatically tucked away for future use. Every little bit of practice results in better drawings next time.

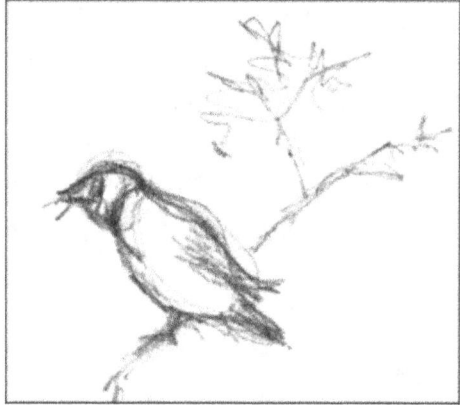

Do this in spare moments by selecting something that looks easy in a book/magazine or from your immediate surroundings.

This is a scribble of an ornamental angel...

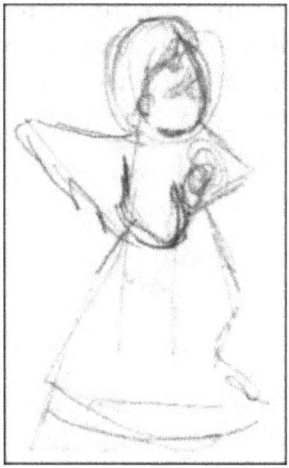

I have a bust of John Wayne, "the Duke", a character from the old Western movies, so I casually scribbled it while sitting at my desk. I'm sure I'll do better next time!

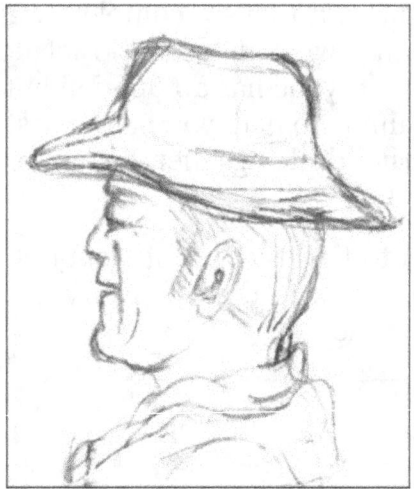

The next image is one I copied from a Japanese artist. I love it due to the basic line used and it only took a couple of seconds to create. There is more information about Japanese artists in Chapter 35.

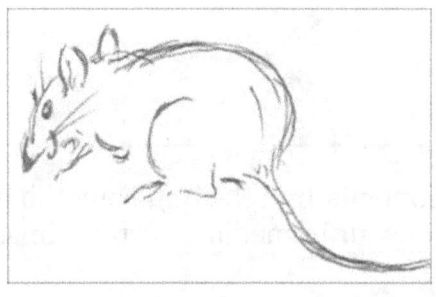

Scribble everything around you.

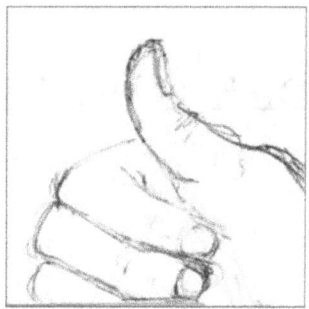

I do this often but my fussiness practically screams at me when I have the intention to scribble yet I end up with something like this...

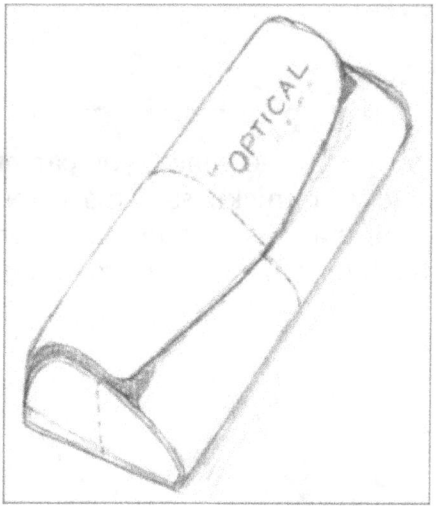

At the time, it was very clear that I still had more work to do with letting go. However, I did learn a few things observation-wise from that particular drawing and that's the main thing.

Scribbling is like doodling except you aim to get a reproduction of a particular object in a short amount of time.

When you say to yourself that you're going to scribble, you actually allow anything to happen on paper and there are no repercussions or damage to ego.

33 - ADDING HIGHLIGHTS

This simple technique is perfect for a trainee artist to effortlessly inject more interest into their artwork. It also proves to be wonderful encouragement at a crucial early stage.

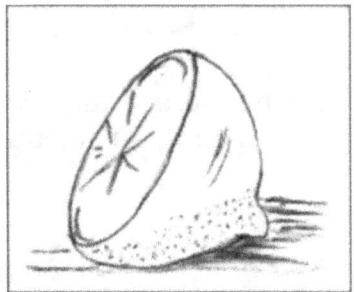

Just by applying pressure on the pencil, you can create a heavier line to portray a sense of shadow or thickness. This transforms a simple little outline into an illustration that has greater character. In other words, you get to add a personal touch to make that image unique.

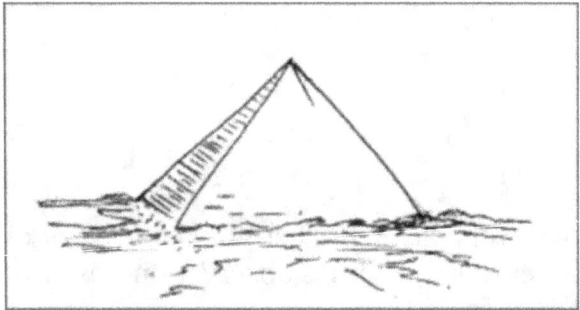

When we talk, we emphasize particular words to get our message across and the same applies to drawing, by placing emphasis on certain portions of a picture to give life and generate interest.

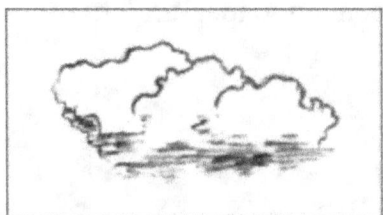

There are 3 basic areas to highlight:

1. Items closest to you

2. The shadow side

3. The bottom of objects

These suggestions provide a good foundation for a start but you're certainly not restricted to them. Doing some experiments helps you discover what appeals to you the most.

As you go over an initial outline, darken lines on the closest objects to make them more prominent so an observer automatically gets the sense of those items being in the foreground.

The shadow side or bottom of a subject is simply depicted with a darker or thicker line -- a 6B pencil is perfect for this job.

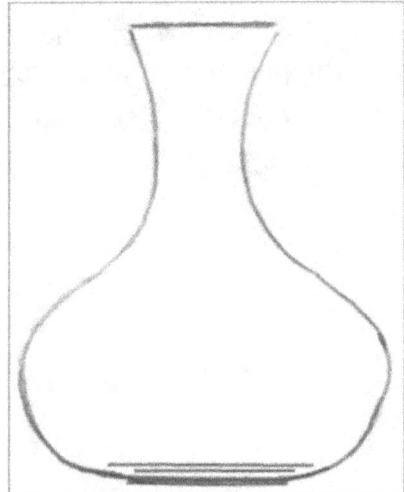

Even though the above image was created while practicing some basic symmetrical shapes, I placed a heavy line to depict the base and then added a couple of strokes above it to give the impression of a shadow. This was back when I was first fiddling with the concept of accent lines and trying to inject my own touch.

As the artist, you get to decide which direction the light comes from and that decision should be made before you start any drawing. A quick study of your chosen topic should reveal some kind of shadow so you naturally make the light source opposite that.

Make sure shadows are on the same side of individual items in a picture.

If you're copying a drawing, the groundwork for shading is already done for you and you can see where to add extra pressure and where to have a feather light touch. Just the fact that you now notice these things puts you one step closer to your goal of drawing efficiently.

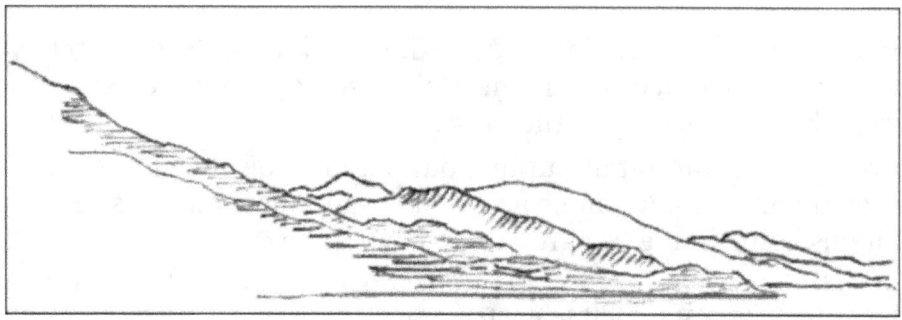

You eventually come to "feel" where you want to add highlights. Just as a dancer choreographs a routine to move in time with music, if you are in tune with the movement of the pencil, you will surely create beautiful art.

In a larger drawing with many objects, you can use a heavier stroke on whatever attracts you and make everything else insignificant by using a lighter stroke.

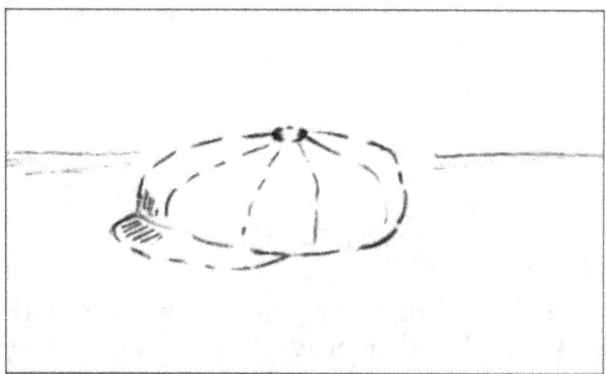

It doesn't matter if you draw attention to the wrong lines because you learn (and remember) with this kind of practice. All mistakes contain lessons and they're good for you!

Plain tree trunks are an excellent subject for this exercise. The simple outline on the left is a typical example that beginners use for practice. The image on the right shows darker lines added on the right side, to give the impression of shadow.

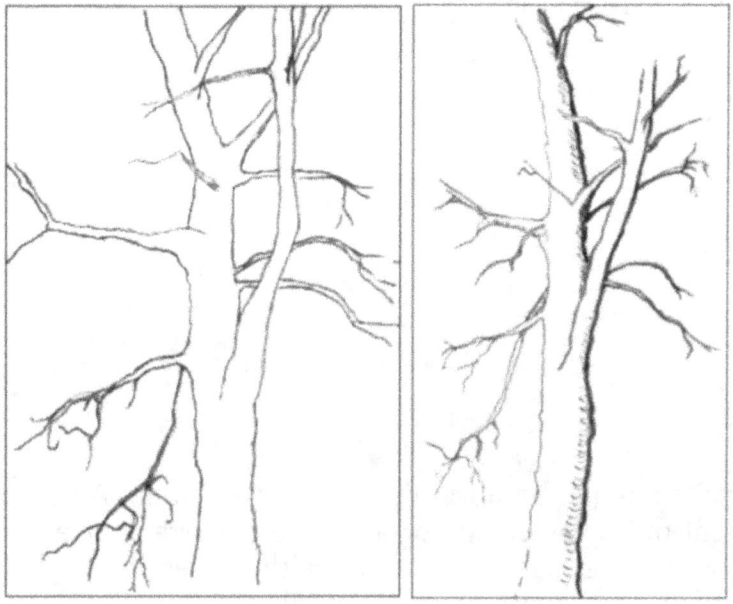

See how suddenly an ordinary outline becomes more visually attractive just by adding pressure to a single line? The best thing is that it only takes a couple of extra seconds of your time.

Accentuating lines can also be used as a type of shading and therefore it invokes your intuition towards knowing where to shade and blend in future work.

As you draw, follow any urges you have to add in more lines along the way. There's no harm done and you can always decide later whether you like it or not. Experimenting is a good way to find what pleases you most.

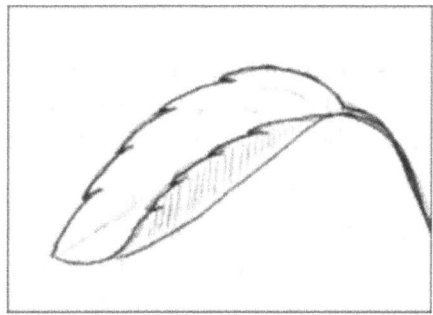

If you draw an item that is folded in some way (like a curled leaf or clothing, for example), just add some small strokes on the underside to give the perception that it is in shadow.

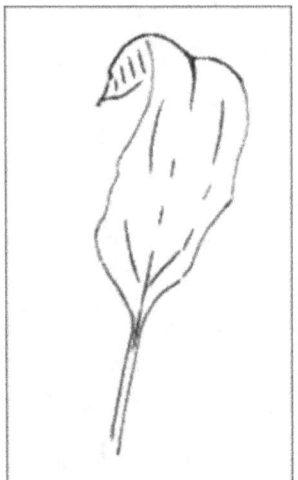

I love this technique because it's not overwhelming. All it consists of is the placement of a heavier line or a couple of extra strokes and that's it. With a bit of practice, patience and a healthy aspect for experimentation, you will learn and grow without even realizing it.

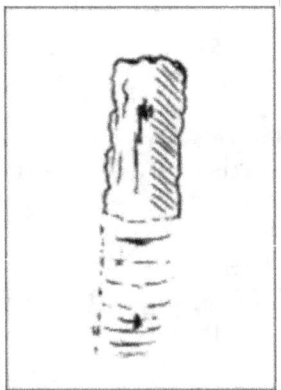

In the outline of a post above, the uneven top is darkened along with some lines on the right to indicate the shadowed side. A couple of lines and dots in the foreground give the perception of a reflection in water.

Use this opportunity to see how far you can take a plain contour and make it into something special. This kind of practice also helps you to understand more about form and that knowledge stands you in good stead forever.

34 - STIPPLING

Stippling is a sequence of dots used to portray shade and forms. This technique is fantastic for trainee artists because tiny dots offer a sense of freedom to create a subject in any way. Once you see credible images, you grow more confident and can adapt to using solid lines without hesitation.

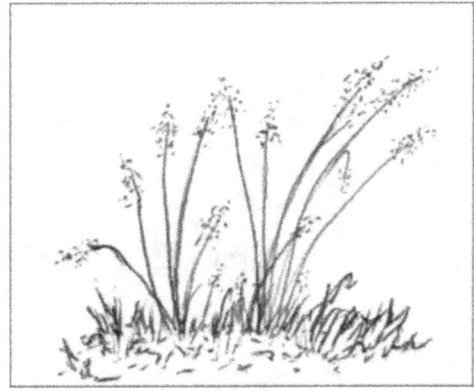

I love doodling with stippling. You can create weeds with a couple of curved lines grouped together and stipple around the tops to depict foliage. The ground consists of a mixture of dots and short dashes.

You get immediate satisfaction yet it takes only seconds to produce. This is something I learned in my beginner days and it's so easy to remember!

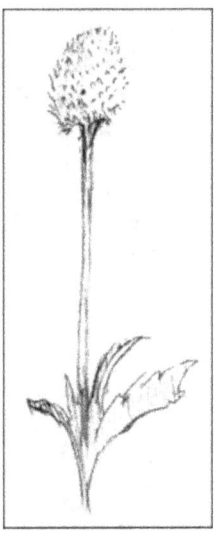

Stippling is best done with any B pencil because they are the softest graphite. H pencils are hard and light, and not really compatible. A fine felt tip pen is best for producing a large, stippled drawing.

When using pencil, make effective dots on paper by holding your pencil upright. I usually choose a 4B pencil (preferably blunt) to make good, dark dots.

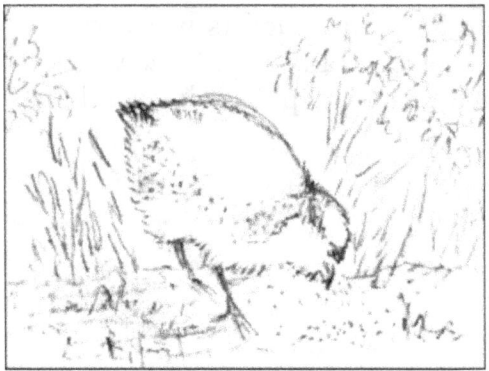

Stippling is great to use in any drawing, along with some idle strokes that somehow form a picture.

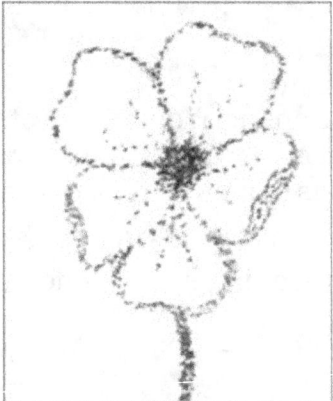

The flower above was done while doodling and the dots were placed wherever I felt they belonged. It doesn't matter what kind of image evolves, just jot some dots and see what happens.

A series of stippled dots is a fantastic way to create an outline and then it's only a matter of completing the drawing in a dot to dot fashion.

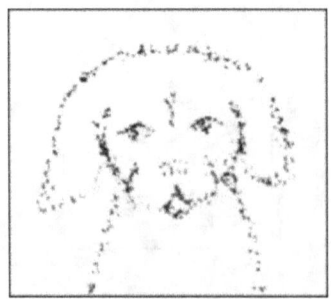

I made up the dog so it's a "Bitza" which is Australian slang for a dog of mixed breeds (short for bits of everything :)

When done lightly, dots are easy to draw over so no erasing is necessary if you want to convert them into solid lines. I urge you to try creating an outline with only dots so you experience how easy it is to get a good likeness.

The art of stippling also comes in handy to draw more complex subjects. I decided to draw a glass which has a couple of tricky bits -- the first is to create a reasonable ellipse shape at the top and the second is to arrive at the same shapely bulge on each side of the glass.

I usually do a few freehand drawings first, to get the feel of the object without using any aids (image below). Just by poking around with lines, you become more familiar with the shape which helps when you settle in to draw it properly.

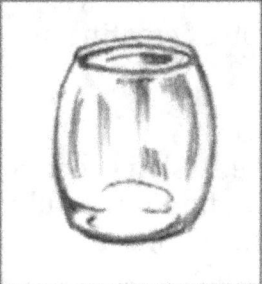

Of course, that's just one of many that I drew roughly – I'm not going to show the worst ones, I do have some pride :)

Since I wasn't entirely happy with the ellipse, I chose to practice drawing more of them to get comfortable with that shape. This is the most successful (and easiest) way I know...

How To Draw An Ellipse:

Start by drawing a very light horizontal line to represent the width. Next, estimate the center of that line and place 2 dots at equal distance on opposite sides (one above and one below) - shown as (A) in the diagram.

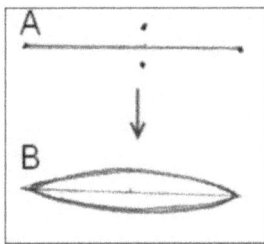

The next step (B) is to join the dots to form a kind of leaf shape.

Draw small curves inside each pointy end (see following image) to make them appear rounded. If you've kept your lines light, it's no trouble to erase the pointed ends.

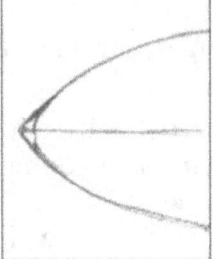

To achieve a larger ellipse, simply place the center dots further away from the line or move them closer to make narrower ones.

When you get used to drawing ellipses, you won't need to draw in the horizontal line but the dot markers will always come in handy. This method does a pretty good job of creating an ellipse – it works for me so I hope it helps you!

Stippling as a Training Aid:

Getting the correct (curved) shape on both sides of a glass can be frustrating so beginners might find it helpful to first create a rectangle and use a series of dots to form the outline around it.

In the image below, 2 parallel, upright lines act as a guide and halfway dots (same distance from vertical line on each side) indicate the widest point of the bulge.

Use as many dots as you wish to create the whole outline. Do the dots light enough so you can see them, don't press hard otherwise it indents the paper and makes it very hard to erase.

This is darkened for the purpose of illustration...

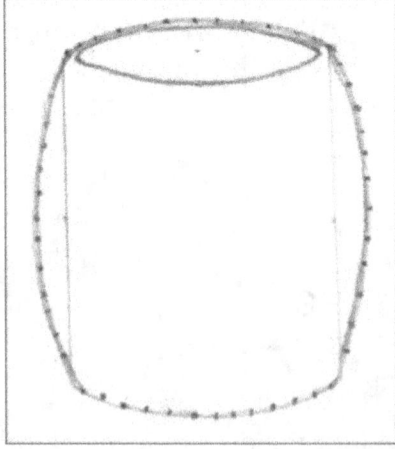

Ok, I went a bit overboard with the dots but hopefully you get the idea.

For the evenly curved sides, you might notice I used the same theory for creating one half of an ellipse on each side of the glass. Experimenting helps you find solutions in the quickest time.

In the finished drawing below, you'd never know I used little dots to help me achieve what I think is pretty close to proportion. The art of stippling leads you towards creating images of all descriptions.

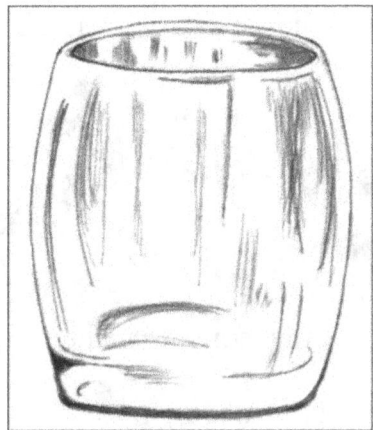

You can make measurements if you want to, that helps everyone in the beginning and after a short while you learn to gauge distances. It's like cooking, everyone follows a recipe at first and after some practice, it becomes normal to guess amounts required.

An added benefit of stippling is its use for shading -- different sized dots and the way they are spaced gives different effects. For example, you can add a gray tone just by regularly spacing marks or for a heavier tone place dots closer together. In the next drawing, dots are used sparingly to give a nice finish.

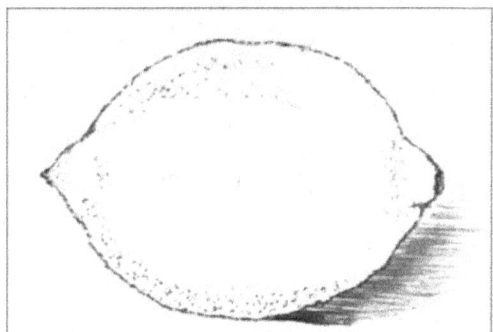

These tiny stipple markings suggest form, shape, depth and contrast but they also convey light and shadow. It's a wonderful addition to any artist's kit bag so please take the time to experiment and see what you can achieve.

35 - SIMPLE JAPANESE ART

In my opinion, Japanese Artists were absolute Masters of line art. Even in its simplicity, every stroke has a purpose and I think their images are captivating.

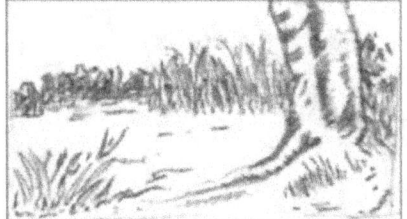

The examples here are my copies of their drawings that I did for practice and enjoyment.

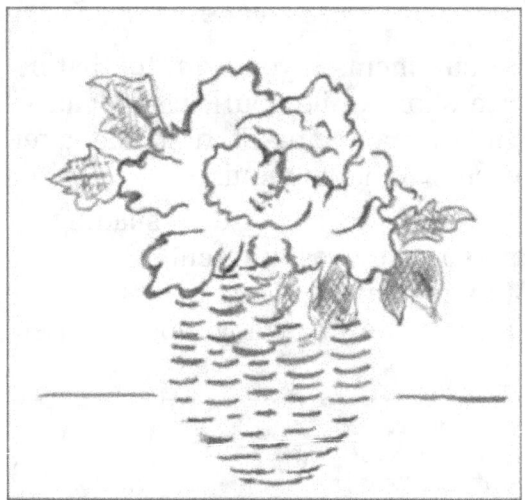

The Japanese masters left behind precise and direct drawings of every natural or artificial object existing in their country.

The following drawings depict some reeds at the water's edge – simple but effectively done.

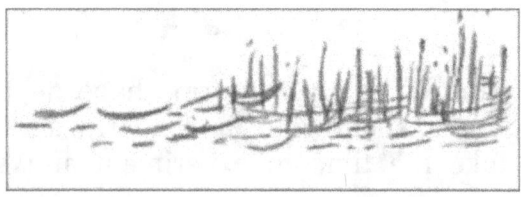

I use a 3B wood pencil to gain a thicker stroke where required.

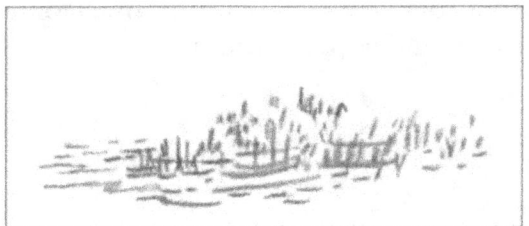

Japanese artists are amazing the way they draw animals with so few lines...

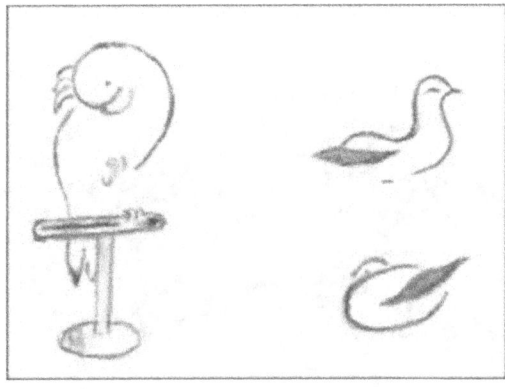

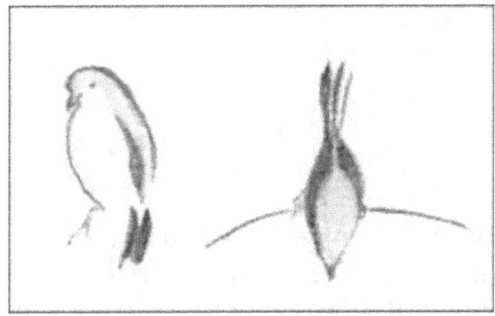

They carefully judge what is best left out and what to include in landscapes.

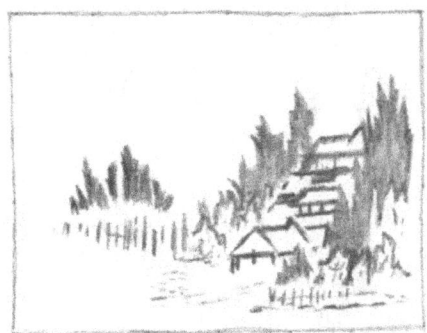

They don't aspire towards photographic artwork, instead they draw what they feel in order to attain individual impressions. That's also what I want so I enjoy studying and copying them.

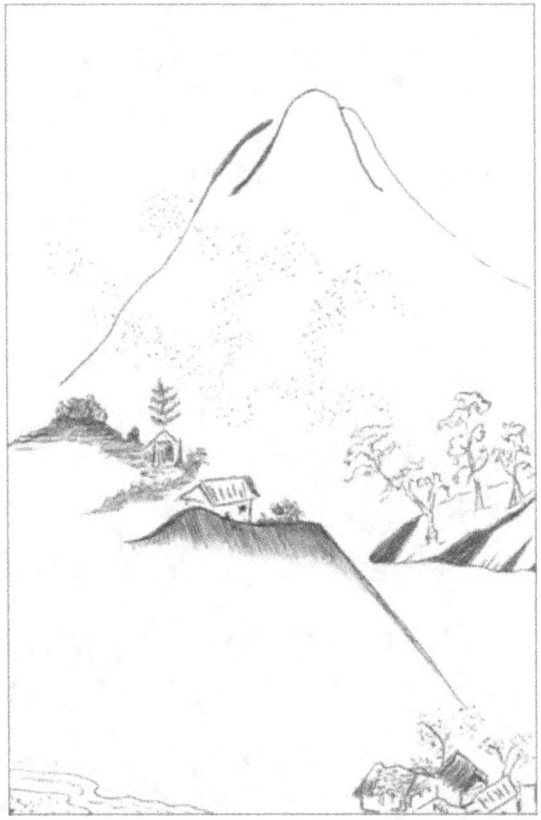

I never feel guilty about copying because that was how I learned to print, skip, dance, ride a bike and so on. Every one of us learns by copying and once we get the hang of it, we don't need to copy any longer.

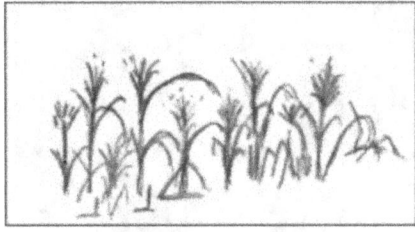

If you're serious about learning to draw, copying is one surefire way to achieve that goal so don't be ashamed to do it.

The next Japanese drawing is from one of my sketchbooks so the texture is different to the photocopy paper used in most other drawings.

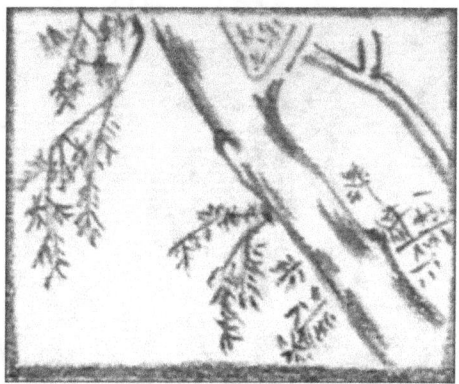

Japanese artists project Nature in such a beautiful way.

It's so simple, I draw a lot of Japanese art on birthday cards.

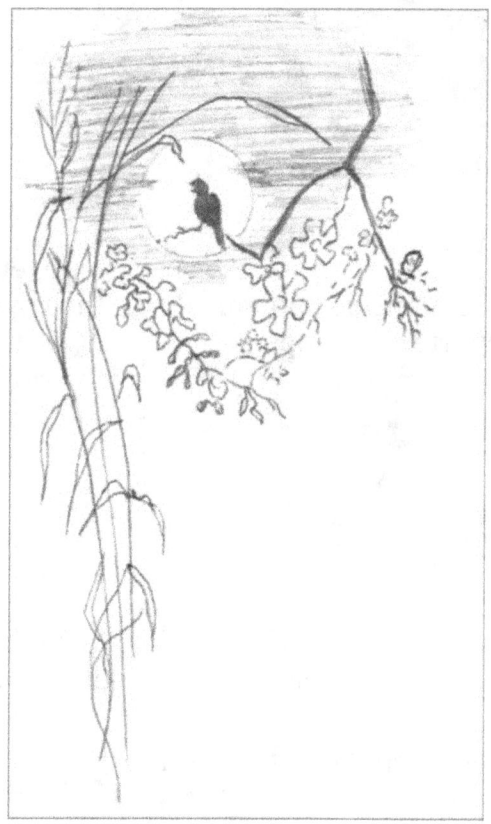

They do great silhouettes so naturally I was prompted to copy them...

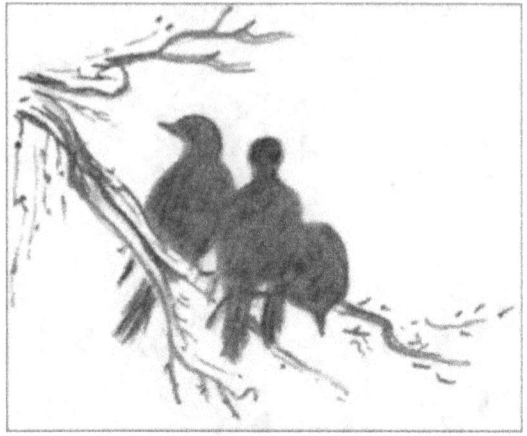

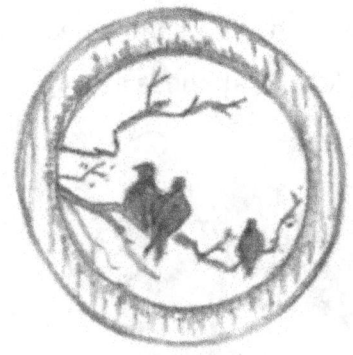

As part of their training, Japanese artists are encouraged to draw everything around them, inside and outside, so their sketchbooks were full of every conceivable form and shape.

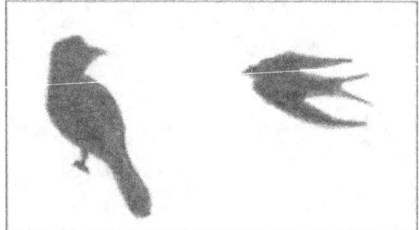

I know it's hard to practice sketching every single thing you see because it's unknown how the sketches will turn out and for some crazy reason we are reluctant to fail.

To overcome this problem, all you have to do is keep a secret sketchbook (or use scraps of paper to throw away) especially for this type of practice. No one ever needs to see it but it is so worthwhile because it's actually how you improve and progress to a total state of confidence in yourself.

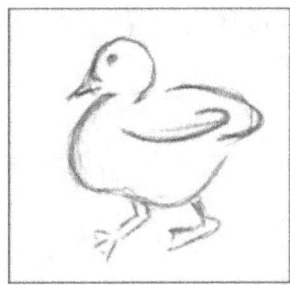

When you're practicing and you decide beforehand that all drawings are to be destroyed, use that opportunity to go over and over lines until you feel the rhythm of the line used in the creation. It's surprising how often these drawings turn out great, so of course you keep those ones.

The next illustration is an original by a Japanese artist and it demonstrates the strokes used to create mountain tops.

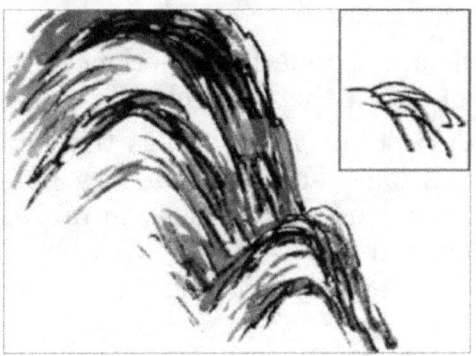

They are taught to find something familiar in their subjects to help them portray an image. In the painting below, the artist saw the shape of a fish in the leaves –

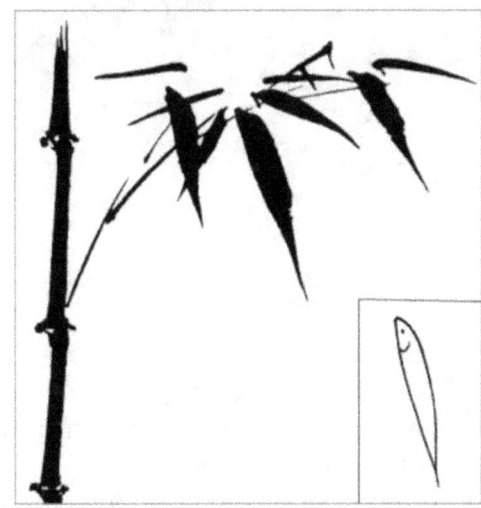

A lot of their art is done with a fine paintbrush but I still see value in copying it with a pencil or pen.

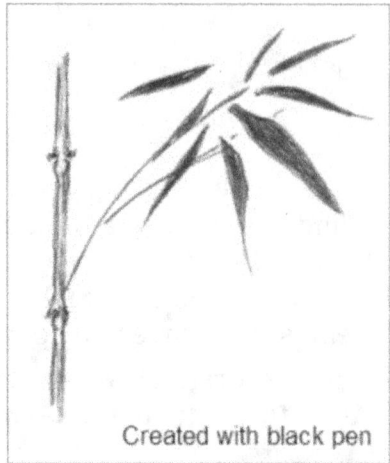

Created with black pen

Drawing with pen is a wonderful experience, it teaches you to put thought into each stroke since there's no chance of erasing.

Japanese artists incorporate many things that tell a story and one of those is weather conditions. For example - to portray bamboo in fair weather, the leaves are spread out joyously; in rainy weather the bamboo leaves hang down despondently; in windy weather the leaves cross each other confusedly, and in the early morning they point upwards to greet the sun.

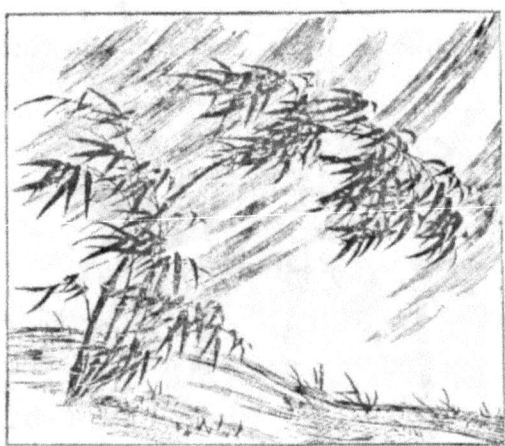

My copies are always (intentionally) different and maybe they don't conform to 'art rules' but that's of no concern to me. Throw out the rule book and just draw! You need to make your own guidelines; please don't be swayed by do's and don'ts from anyone.

All Master Artists cultivated their own style and ignored traditional laws. They were criticized of course, but luckily they stayed true to what they liked and eventually their unique ability was recognized.

36 - THUMBNAIL DRAWINGS

In the art world, thumbnail size can be anything from one inch through to possibly 3 inch squares. My preference is 1½ inch squares but the choice is yours for whatever size.

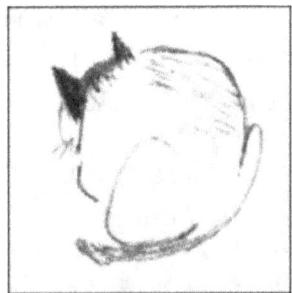

A sheet of thumbnails is best done on an A5 piece of paper (half a standard letter size) especially if you're impatient (like me) to see a finished page. It's very satisfying browsing completed pages of thumbnails and enjoying all the individual images.

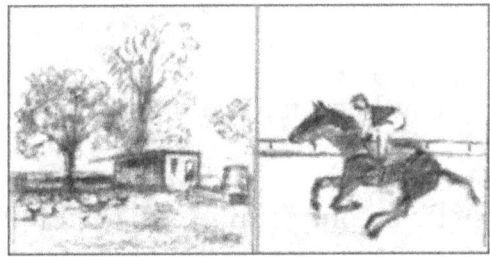

My pages are a real mish-mash of assorted images with no real consistent theme because I draw what appeals to me at the time.

When you experiment with drawing inside a small square, you're forced to omit fussy details and look only for the major "players" in a scene. This practice is very beneficial for your artistic growth.

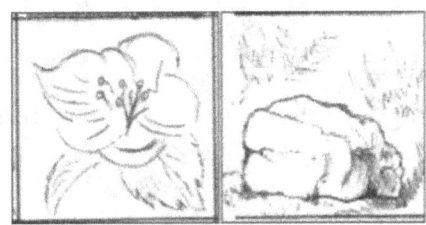

Thumbnail sketches are used by artists to quickly capture an impression or an idea, like in the images below.

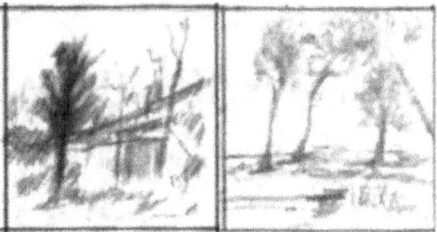

You can omit or include anything in a drawing -- you are in control at all times and thumbnails are the perfect thing to help you decide.

All you need to do is first *lightly* sketch your image into the square to make sure it all fits into that space. Use an eraser as much as you like because this initial light sketch will save you a lot of time and frustration.

A good outline results in a good image.

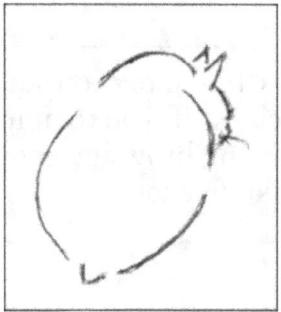

Once you have rough outlines in place, study the reference picture again and proceed to mark in light and dark areas. It's hard to say what method you will adopt because we are each so different in our chosen approach. I took a long time to settle on one routine and even today I still love to try different things.

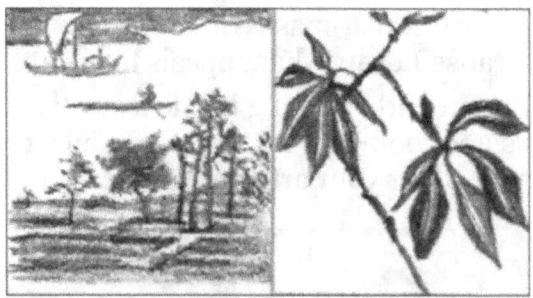

A thumbnail sketch generally only takes a minute or two to complete. It doesn't matter how it turns out, the point is you gain more experience and/or sureness with every single stroke. You become more aware of existing skills and that gives you impetus to continue challenging yourself.

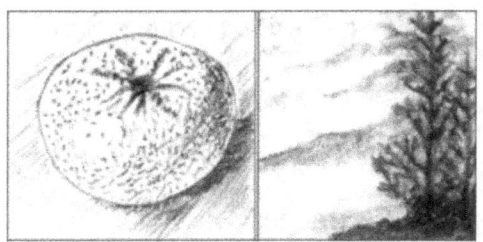

As always, take this opportunity to experiment with different drawing methods in a small area. The left image is stippled and the right is done with the side of the pencil (from a photo of the Smoky Mountains in USA).

You have nothing to lose by trying and there are many rewards, like making discoveries that ultimately form your unique style.

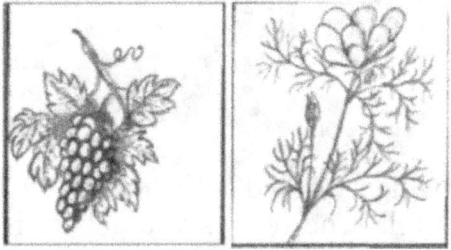

If you have an aversion to drawing outdoors, it's completely fine to use reference photos/pictures otherwise you'd never get to draw and what's the point of that? Do what works for you and ignore what people think or say on the matter. You are the number one priority and if you have a desire to draw, you need to do everything that feels right in order for it to happen.

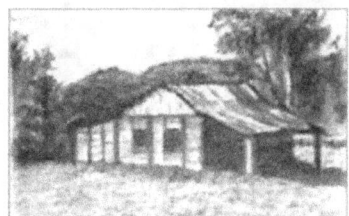

Collect pictures that inspire you to draw. Times of motivation or inspiration are spasmodic but by having a handy collection ready, it saves that special moment from being lost. I often cut pictures out of magazines or junk mail and I've discovered how it really depends on that future point in time whether I want to draw it or not.

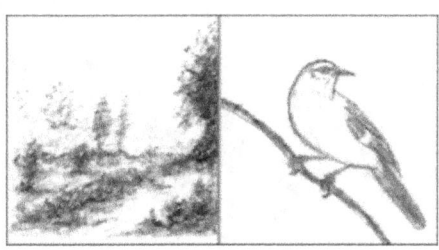

Always draw subjects that interest you. Anytime you catch yourself drawing something in your mind, that's a good indication that you'll probably do a decent representation of it. Even if it doesn't turn out the way you'd like, that little bit of extra practice moves you closer to your goal so it's not a wasted effort.

Copy other artists because images are already pared down to basic lines and show how to represent things, rather than you struggling and wondering how to convert a complex scene into a drawing. Why re-invent the wheel when someone has already done it for you?

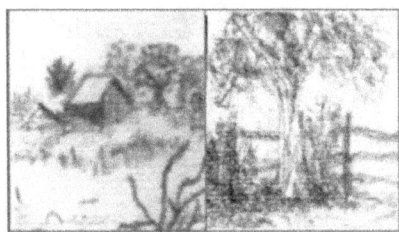

Copying other drawings worked well for me so I hope you have the same success story to tell! The results you get from this type of practice gives you the boost you need to continue.

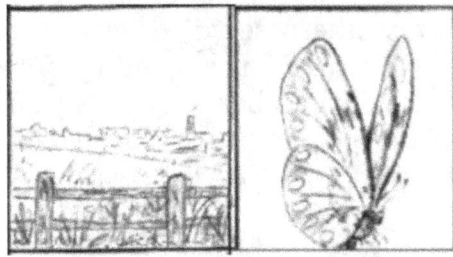

When copying other artists, please make a note of who you copied and the current date. This is a reminder that the drawing is not yours and you don't make the mistake of ever claiming or selling it as an original by you. That comes in handy when you forget you were once reliant on someone else's guidance.

Put notes on an adjoining page or on the back but take care your writing doesn't penetrate through to the other side and ruin your artwork.

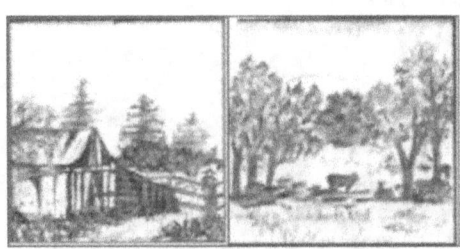

Nothing compares to the satisfaction you feel once you achieve a good drawing and if that happens only after copying someone else's artwork, then continue to do it until you can accomplish it on your own.

I remember when I copied a boat from a Thailand tourism photo in the paper -- I stared at it for ages, absolutely stunned that it turned out ok. This is what happens when you are persistent.

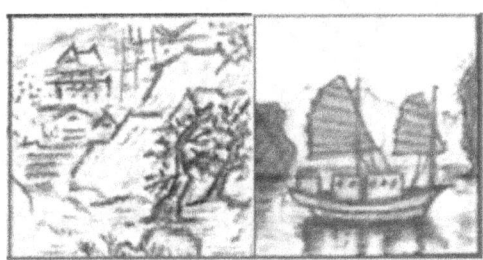

From that moment on, my enthusiasm stayed high and drawing improved quickly. In hindsight, I realize thumbnail-sized drawings particularly helped me to understand and grasp the techniques of proportion and perspective.

On the 40th anniversary of the first moon walk. I drew a thumbnail to honor that event and I scrawled the date, 20 July '09, in the bottom left corner.

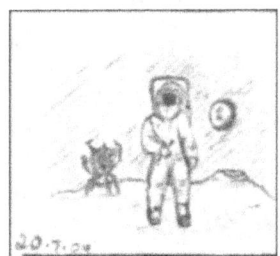

Every single one of us can draw -- if we desire it! You don't have to have a special talent; all you have to have is patience as you continue to draw one thing after another.

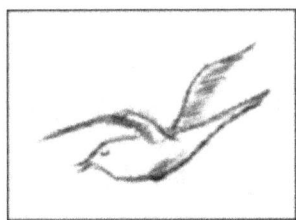

Below you can see one of my thumbnail pages, enlarged for better viewing...

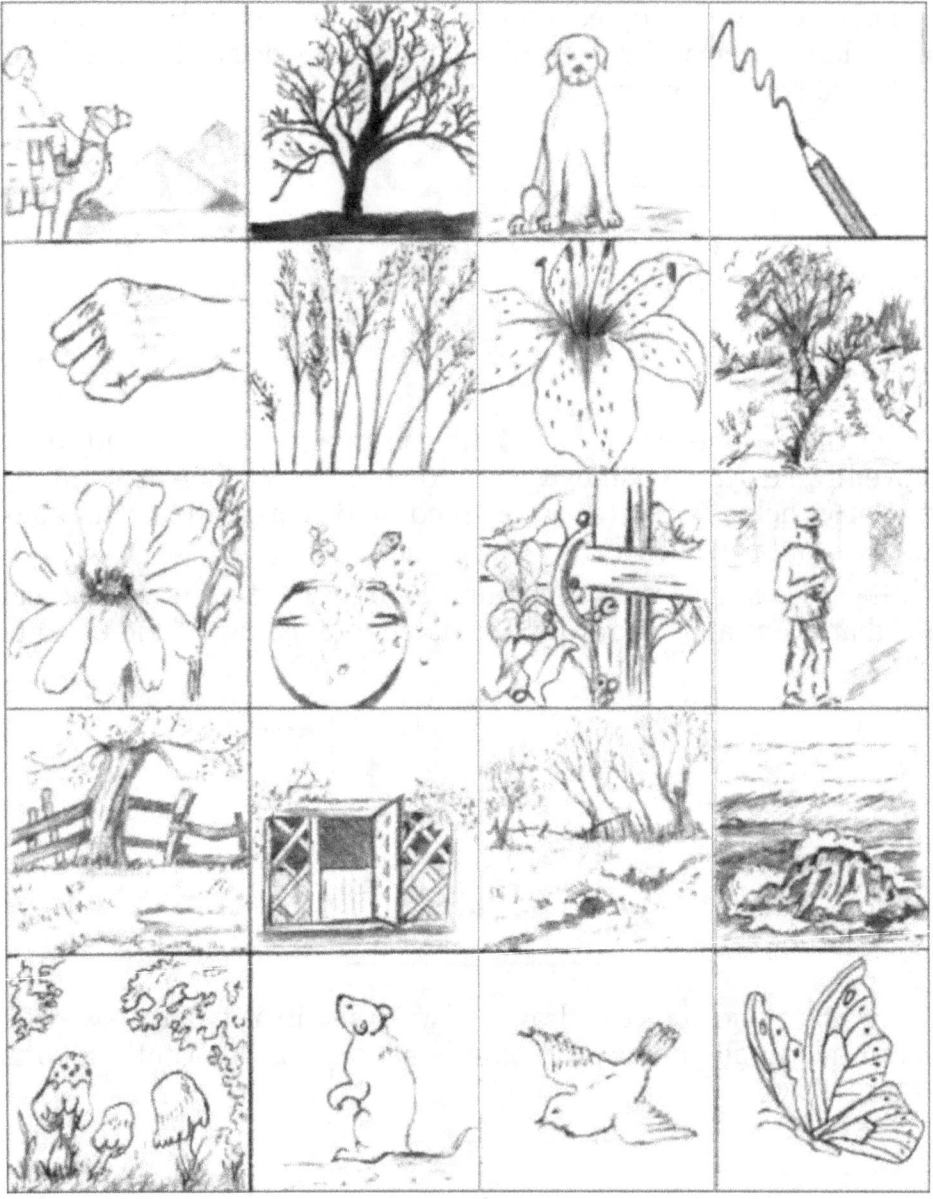

Anything can be accomplished if you think it is even remotely possible.

37 - CONCLUSION

If you completed every exercise in Book 1 – "Drawing Lessons", I congratulate you for your persistence and willingness -- that really is a grand achievement.

The basic information in that section is merely a stepping stone towards your participation in a great drawing adventure. By starting with simple procedures, you can progress steadily and with surety.

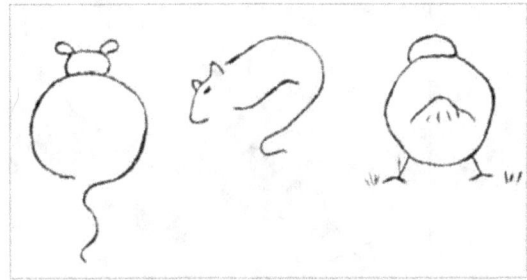

Once the groundwork is done, your artistic road ahead is now smoother than it was yesterday and you're ready to go an extra mile with Book 2 – "How To Draw Outlines" which represents my initial learning experience. I attribute those methods to my success to rapidly grow as an artist.

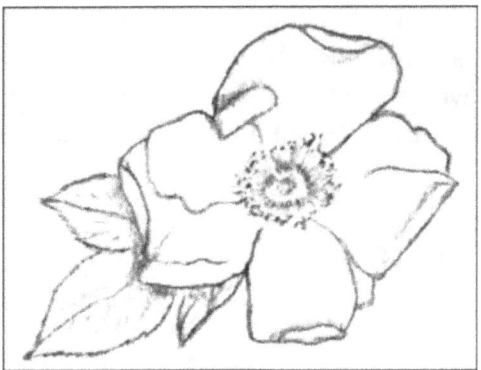

You have the resources within you to make great drawings, all you need to do is implement the steps detailed here and you're on your way -- it really is that simple. Once you have a clear idea of how to compose an initial draft or outline, you will never have uncertain moments with a pencil again.

Dedicate time to thoroughly learn each step before moving to the next stage and your progression will go smoothly. The fun is in the journey so allow your spirit the freedom to do whatever it visualizes.

In Book 3 - "Drawing and Sketching Nature", you are shown how to construct images using all the combined elements in art.

Once you make these abilities a habit, the energy you apply to each stroke becomes obvious in your spontaneous sketches. The subject of Nature isn't new but the way you illustrate it is fresh and therefore undoubtedly attractive.

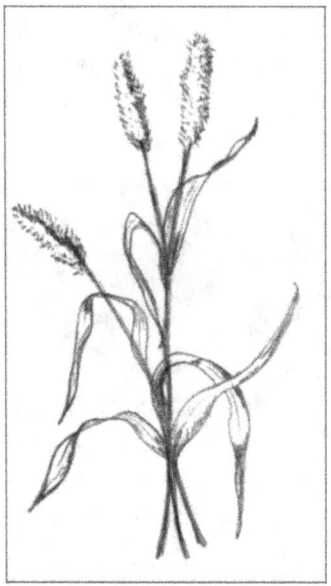

As hobby artists, we all strive to draw directly from a subject and the power to do this develops only through constant practice. There is no doubt that anyone can draw or sketch but they have to have the desire to do so.

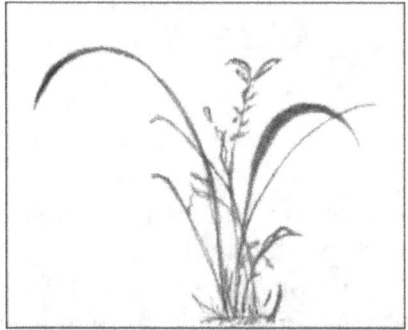

I like to combine both drawing and sketching in my images and that's my preferred style now. It takes a while for your particular style to evolve so please give yourself some time to find your preference.

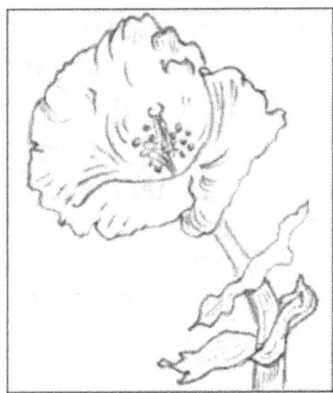

In Book 4 - "Drawing Tips For Beginners", you're shown a variety of ways to produce an image and really it just doesn't matter how you get there. I can show you the way I learned to draw but you are the one who must decide on the path you want to take. Hopefully, if I've done a decent job, this information is all you need to become a very competent hobby artist.

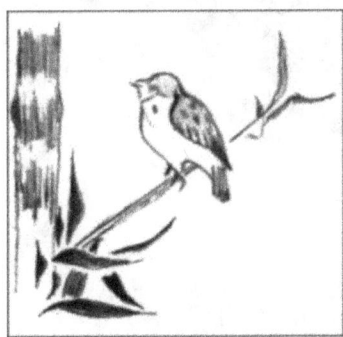

Major points are repeated throughout so you remember them. Repetition is a very important component of drawing.

I'm convinced half the problem with learning to draw is overcoming doubt in our minds. Even if you don't feel confident, continuously pretend you are confident and see what transpires. Eventually, you'll love the feeling and adopt that attitude all the time!

Another important element is patience. Giving up is easy but if you really want to draw, persevere and practice whenever you can. If you have the patience, you will succeed.

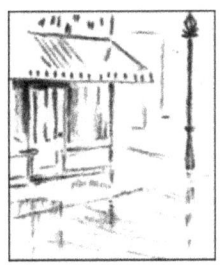

There is no right or wrong in drawing so what are you waiting for? You are restricted only by your own (self-imposed) limitations. You do have the potential to do anything you want, you just have to be open to discovering it!

When I browse through my beginner practice pages, I am still amazed at some of the work I produced even though I had never drawn anything recognizable in my 40+ years. It was those initial results that spurred me on with great momentum because I wanted to experience more of that euphoria. I did tell you it's an addiction, didn't I?

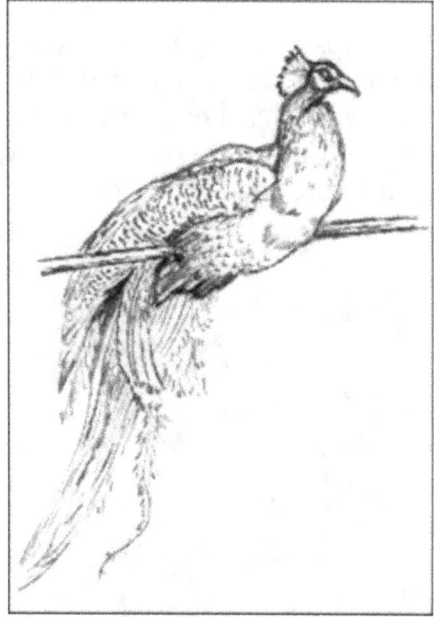

Remember not to worry about what people think. Being self-conscious about that holds you back from being who you want to be.

Also, do what you can to avoid being self-critical. I don't know why we torture ourselves and become discouraged so easily but it happens to a good majority of us. Learn to accept every piece you create and take the time to acknowledge your personal achievements. Everybody starts at the beginning!

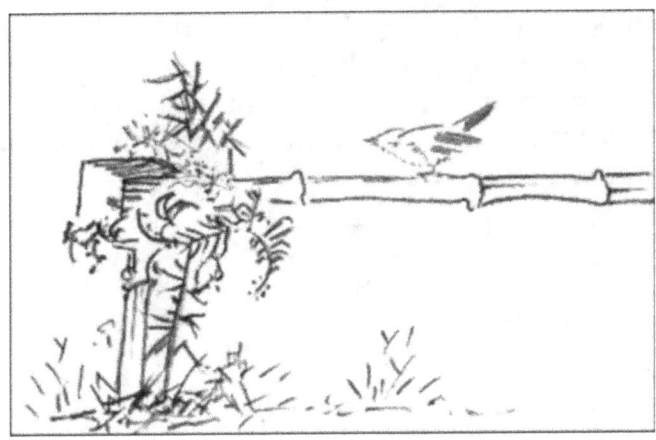

To learn to draw doesn't necessarily mean you have to be able to draw everything. Follow your heart and instinct to draw your favorite subject because then you will effortlessly learn everything you need to know.

Allow and accept mistakes – it's just not normal if you do everything perfectly first time!

Make your own rules, please yourself what you draw and how you draw it; by all means draw in ignorance - it's fun! Who cares if you don't understand perspective or if you don't add light and shade in your drawings? If you're happy, that's all that matters.

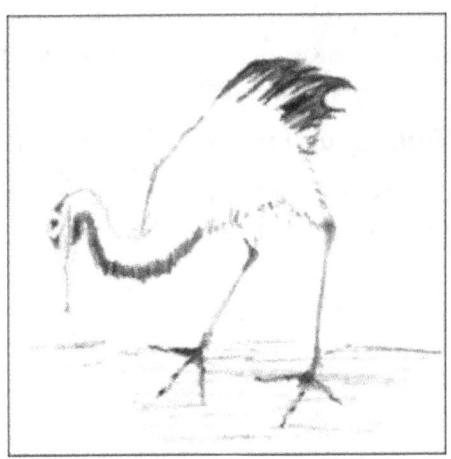

Drawing is a hobby that encourages freedom of expression. Experience the joys of drawing and while you're doing that, you're learning all the time!

Sure, I don't explain the complexities or theories of perspective or proportion but I haven't read anything (and I've read a lot!) that makes those processes easy to understand. Instead, just let your eyes guide you along and with a little assistance from the tips divulged here, you will achieve good proportions anyway.

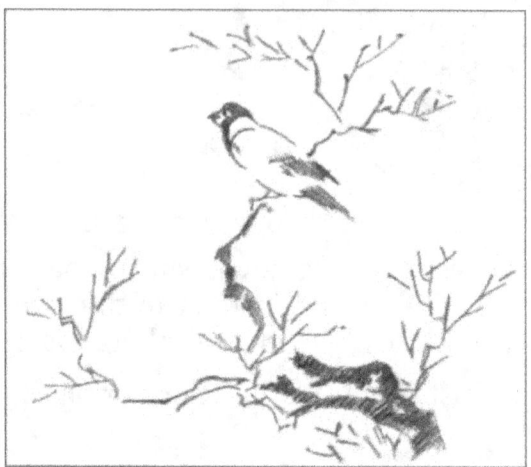

I don't go into detail about drawing supplies or materials because your preferences will evolve with time and experimentation. All it takes to learn to draw is any kind of pencil, paper and eraser - simple.

To succeed in anything, we must persevere and be determined to continue practicing regardless of any difficulties that may arise. This quote by Maya Angelou pretty much sums it up:

'Nothing will work unless you do.'

Let yourself be free with your pencil, be curious and watch what happens when you don't try to interfere with the ensuing result.

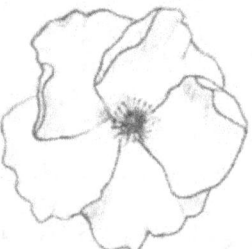

It is with great pleasure that I share my revelations with you, in the hope that you can teach your family and friends in the same manner. There is no reason why anyone should not know how to draw, it's as familiar as writing and talking and all it takes is repetition to master it.

If you want to be a professional artist, I encourage you to seek someone who has the required knowledge or to enroll in college to take you where you want to be. Nothing pleases me more than when I hear from people who started by following my advice and they go on to draw commissioned works of art! The choice is all yours.

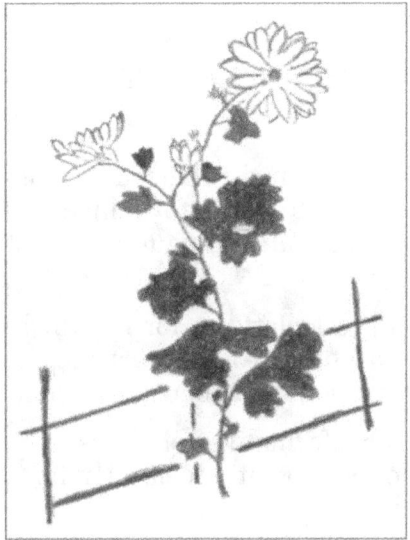

Drawing is an escape from stress and when you emerge from that space in time where nothing matters, you are left with feelings of satisfaction, confidence and well-being. I can't recommend it highly enough, it's very good for your state of health.

Be happy and content, you only get one chance at life so make it everything you want it to be.

I wish you great success - may you have many fascinating drawing days that enrich your life beyond all expectations!

Confidence comes not from always being right but from not fearing to be wrong. - Peter T. McIntyre

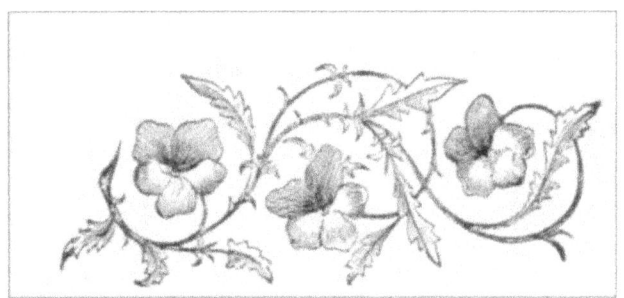

ABOUT THE AUTHOR

When Author Kate Berry taught herself to draw, she stripped down complicated theory and converted it into simple and achievable steps. This strategy proved to be so successful, she figured it would be selfish to keep that knowledge to herself.

Kindle books offered a great platform for her to share the drawing tips and techniques that worked the best. To her surprise, a couple of them became Number One Best Sellers and suddenly there was a demand for printed versions.

Kate's intention with this informative volume is to help you discover what you can create despite self-doubts and it's really her honor to share this amazing experience with you.

Kate recommends visiting allaboutdrawings.com to find a huge selection of simple illustrations and instructions that are free for everyone.

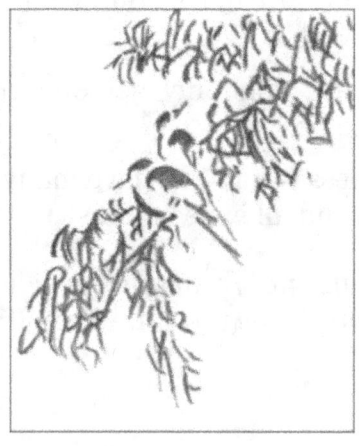

www.ingramcontent.com/pod-product-compliance
Lightning Source LLC
Chambersburg PA
CBHW080810180526
45168CB00006B/2389

* 9 7 8 1 5 0 8 4 4 2 9 7 4 *